Anne Hutchinson

A Captivating Guide to the Puritan Leader in Colonial Massachusetts Who Is Considered to Be One of the Earliest American Feminists

Free Bonus from Captivating History (Available for a Limited time)

Hi History Lovers!

Now you have a chance to join our exclusive history list so you can get your first history ebook for free as well as discounts and a potential to get more history books for free! Simply visit the link below to join.

Captivatinghistory.com/ebook

Also, make sure to follow us on Facebook, Twitter and Youtube by searching for Captivating History.

Contents

Introduction

Her steps were determined and steady, even though the plank of the wooden ship bobbed up and down in the glittering but frigid water that splashed against the wet dock. In the first light of day, these were the times tinged with the hues of promise shadowed only by the vague unknown. Anne Hutchinson was just a follower, or so she thought, but she had many queued up behind her as she followed her spiritual mentor to Boston in the early days of the Massachusetts Bay Colony.

An older grave man in grey stood at the door of a roughly-hewn white-washed church. Reverend John Cotton spoke only in muted tones of love and encouragement. The people smiled and nodded as they gleefully filed past him and entered the solace of his church. With the pitter-patter sounds of the little feet of Anne's children and her husband's warm body beside her, Anne Hutchinson feels as if she's home.

The unity of their faith was like a light that guided these fervent Puritans. It was comforting to note that one's long-held religious beliefs were united with the towns that now welcomed them. Back in their homeland of Europe, their stiff, pompous church prelates couldn't handle any deviation from their staunch and ancient ways. There was no room for flexibility in England, which included thought-provoking religious reforms. However, the Puritans reproduced all the trappings of the Old World into the New World they now resided in. It was a world in which both the civic and religious government blended together in an awkward way. This was the virgin soil into which was planted the theological factions—the free grace advocates, the Antinomians, and the reformed theologians of the Protestant Reformation.

Although sometimes labeled as a feminist, Anne Hutchinson didn't blow her trumpet about women's issues. She played the horn about issues that meant something to those with eternal passions and who had tasted the victories rendered by their steadfast theological beliefs. When the hoary heads of the prejudiced jerked up with fits of venial words like "seducer," "whore," or "temptress," she heard them not. Who should pay heed to such meaningless prattle? Like her father, Francis Marbury, Anne Hutchinson was logically practical.

Only in the darkness of the unexplained shadows that had crossed various parts of this land before her and her followers were those who trod before, like John Winthrop and Thomas Dudley and about one thousand Puritan settlers. They had a charter to found the land and fashion a system of beliefs that matched those they had left behind in England, claiming they wanted religious reform. John Cotton eventually flowed with the tide, but Hutchinson didn't. She spoke for herself without parroting others, and other religious leaders wanted to understand the value of her words and compare them with the doctrine they had learned. No woman had ever related to them on their own level. However, the conservatism of the times couldn't handle her daring, incisive thoughts or her ambitions. She trudged nearly sixty miles on foot to her trial in near-freezing weather and was made to stand in the center of an assembly of men in pointy hats and black cloaks. The judges were supposed to test and judge her for the integrity and purity of her beliefs, but they, who had claimed to have come to America to escape religious persecution, persecuted her. They battered her with questions designed to entrap. Perhaps it was the fact that Anne had a depth of theological knowledge that Puritan society wasn't yet ready to accept from a woman. Or perhaps it was because Anne's beliefs were an aberration of their firmly held doctrines. Yet Anne came to serve and granted her listeners insight. In that lamp-lit, make-shift courtroom, she was made to defend the principles she taught to the members of her little meeting groups, which were modest groups composed mostly of women that the ordained and well-trained clerical judges found to be a threat. In turn, she was banished from her own countrymen and made to walk through unfriendly forests and fields in search of a welcoming refuge. Hers was a journey of determination and love, as she and her flock moved to two colonies. The peace that she finally found was all too briefly felt. Her ending was a bad and bloody one, as she and her family were victimized by the forces of unrelenting history— "because there was no place for them at the inn."

This book tells the story of Anne Hutchinson's life—a life with a mission. Strict chronological sequence isn't adhered to because the content of Hutchinson's message is more thematic. The people in her life didn't appear as if in snapshots but kept reappearing over and over again. Thus, the book is split up into sections to make it easier for the reader living in a different time and place.

Chapter 1 – Ramifications of the Reformation

During the 16th century, the role of religion was intertwined with politics in Europe. For example, kings were expected to get papal permission to marry, and children were baptized by church-sanctioned clerics. Wars were fought (and are still fought) in the name of religion. In 1534, due to a dispute with the pope over permission to marry Anne Boleyn, King Henry VIII broke England's ties with the Catholic Church and founded the Church of England (the Anglican Church). No longer were the British subject to the pope and his mandates in matters of religion. Henry VIII's bold move triggered the English Reformation. In Europe, a parallel movement arose by virtue of the efforts of Martin Luther in Germany. This movement was called the Protestant Reformation. People eschewed being fed doctrine like porridge and began to think for themselves, although within limits. In doing so, people began to analyze and critique the traditional religious teachings uttered from the pulpits, which some felt were mindless drivel and primitive regurgitations of clerical syllabi. That applied not only to the people themselves but also to members of the clergy and even religious scholars.

King Henry VIII's daughter, Queen Elizabeth I, continued his efforts to purify the land of "papist" practices. However, to some, it appeared that she had not cleansed the Anglican religion of many of the vestiges that were still Catholic in appearance and function. Within the umbrella of Anglicanism, movements arose. One was propelled by John Calvin, a French theologian. His belief set was called Calvinism, but it soon took a foothold in Scotland under John Knox, who developed it into Scottish Presbyterianism. It slowly spread southward to the rest of England.

Puritanism wasn't a separate religious sect at that time; it was a movement within the Church of England. Puritans regularly attended religious services at the Anglican churches. Some of those churches were headed by ministers trained in Calvinistic theology, and their homilies and teachings reflected that. During the era of reformed theology, there arose a radical movement called Puritanism. Puritans were critical of some of the extraneous practices and leftover vestiges that could remind congregants of Roman Catholicism. They eschewed the wearing of ornamental vestments by the Anglican clergy, stained glass windows, and the like. Puritans were more stoic than the Anglicans, wore dark clothing, and disapproved of frivolous pastimes that were normally allowed by the Catholics. They also maintained a stricter adherence to the Bible.

Anne Hutchinson's father, Francis Marbury, was a minister who eschewed the use of ornate vestments and the wearing of surplices—a torso-length white cotton garment sometimes bordered in lace and worn over a minister's clothing. He also abandoned many of the ceremonial accouterments that the Anglicans had. Marbury felt that such embellishments were too "Catholic" or "papist." Although he claimed he was "no Puritan," Marbury was very much like a Puritan in his everyday behavior, though he lacked the solemnity they displayed. He was a quick wit with a sarcastic tinge—a characteristic that antagonized the Anglican authorities time and time again.

Marbury ranted for years against the religious prelates for their failure to educate the members of the clergy. He bemoaned the fact that people in the congregation hadn't even learned the Lord's Prayer. Furthermore, he indicated that very little preaching was actually done, and the ignorant clergy members even permitted chickens and pigs to wander around the church during the service! Marbury was a practical man who felt it was ludicrous to permit ministers to preach from a Bible they could barely read. He also criticized the traditional Anglican church, saying it was a "kind of charm" and that people were sometimes persuaded to believe they could "buy" salvation if they could afford to make the donations.

Francis Marbury under Arrest

Marbury bitterly complained about the lack of education of the clergy members and the poor quality of their primitive preaching practices. In 1578, he was taken into court and interrogated by the Bishop of London, John Aylmer, as well as Sir Owen Hopton and Archdeacon John Mullins. Marbury was bold and accused local prelates of the Church of England of having clergy members who were inadequate and ill-prepared when it came to preaching. Like Marbury, Bishop Aylmer was also a "hot-head" and is said to have retorted, "You have taken upon yourself to be a preacher, but there is nothing else in you. You are a very ass, an idiot, and a fool." Because of his non-conforming church practices and his belligerence, Francis Marbury was convicted of heresy and went to Marshalsea Prison for two years. Following his imprisonment, he was assigned a ministry at St. Wilford's Church in Alford, England.

In 1582, he married Elizabeth Moore and became a school teacher. About four years later, his wife died, and within a year, he remarried, this time to Bridget Dryden. History indicates that he had about twenty children. Many of the Marbury descendants were famous figures and include the poet John Dryden, US senator Mitt Romney, and three American presidents—Franklin Delano Roosevelt, George H.W. Bush, and George W. Bush. In 1590, Marbury spoke up again, publicly criticizing the Anglican clergy members for its neglect of clerical training. As a result, he was placed under house arrest and spent many of his days in his garden since he was forbidden to preach or work while his family was struggling to survive. Most likely, they were supported by his in-laws, the Drydens. This was an age when family bloodlines meant the difference between poverty and wealth. After his suspension was lifted, Francis didn't publicly complain about the weaknesses of his Anglican overlords.

His daughter, Anne, was born while her father was under house arrest. There's no record of her birth, but she was baptized in July 1591. Like her father, she was outspoken, opinionated, and courageous. Francis Marbury homeschooled Anne along with her many siblings, which was quite a challenge. Nineteen of his children survived their childhood, despite the presence of the Black Plague. The education of women was just becoming acceptable in the 16th century, as the Queen of England herself spoke six languages. Marbury firmly believed his children should all have a solid education, regardless of their gender, so that they could contribute to society and help their communities progress into a new age. He taught his children using many techniques, including an amusing allegory in which he related his views about the inflated use of power by using the make-believe voice of an ignorant buffoon.

Once Anne's father was allowed to preach again, he and his family moved to London. He moved there because the stricter Puritan beliefs were better tolerated in the city since the population was more heterogeneous. Francis Marbury became a minister at two churches there, as there was a shortage of clergy members at the beginning of the 17th century. He had the ultimate honor of delivering a sermon upon the accession of King James I to the English throne in 1603. Marbury was well-known in his time, and some of his writings have even survived to this day. His name was mentioned by Sir Francis Bacon, a respected scientist who would one day become the Lord Chancellor of England. Bacon affectionately called Marbury "The Preacher," as if there were no others in England.

Role of Women

During the 17th century, women were relegated to tasks such as raising children and cooking. In addition, women were expected to organize the household, sew clothing, take care of the animals, clean, do some outdoor work like picking berries or help to harvest the vegetables, and "keep the home fires burning" in every meaning of the phrase. Men did the heavy work outside the house, helped with the crops, took care of ordering seeds and supplies, organized their businesses, and were expected to wrestle with intellectual concepts related to politics, religion, and affairs of the state. The latter duties were much more than social in nature; they were essential, as they were needed to influence the civic authorities in such a way that it would benefit their families. The world was now beyond the era of depending upon physical prowess for basic survival. Building and maintaining civic and religious communities were essential in reducing the stress of living. The clan mentality no longer propelled society. With regard to politics and religion, most women veiled their opinions in letter writing or confined their speculations within the walls of their homes, like turtles hiding inside their shells. Anne would turn out not to be like that. She would grow to be outspoken and even brutally frank on occasion.

Wisdom in an English Country Town

Anne grew up in Alford, a quaint and humble town that hosted weekly markets in the square and had just a handful of little buildings and shops, like the apothecary, the fabric store, and the church. That was where she met young William Hutchinson, who became the churchwarden in 1620. William Hutchinson, who was described as being gentle and soft-spoken, worked as a clothing merchant. When he moved to London, he prospered extremely well in the business.

When Anne's father was transferred to London, she renewed her friendship with William Hutchinson. It was heartening to find a friendly face and someone who had a common background. When women reached marrying age, they were encouraged to seek out men who could financially support them as well as any children from their union. Women in 17th-century England, particularly those who ascribed to Puritan values, married for love. There were no pre-arranged marriages among the Puritans. They had seen royal families subject themselves to pre-arranged marriages and spend miserable lives together, only to visit their unhappiness upon those whom they ruled.

Most importantly, it was essential that women marry young because society was male-dominated, meaning females could rarely find suitable and sustainable employment by themselves. When Anne's father suddenly died in 1611, she turned to her childhood friend, William Hutchinson, for support, and they married the following year. Marriages weren't elaborate affairs like they are today; they were simple—especially among the Puritans. Since Alford was warm and friendly to Anne and William as children, they moved back there shortly after they were married. Anne's husband was also a devout Christian, and so, the two of them kept abreast of religious matters in the area.

At St. Wilfrid's parish church of Alford, the people chatted about a charismatic preacher by the name of John Cotton, who served in the nearby town of Boston—not to be confused with the city by the same name in the United States. Cotton was a Puritan like Anne and her father, and he was critical of the ostentatious tendencies on the part of the clergy, as they wore ornamental robes and paraded about under the light cast from stained glass windows.

John Cotton's beliefs deviated somewhat from traditional Anglicanism because he emphasized the role of faith and conversion to Christ as opposed to the exclusive reliance on a life of good works for personal salvation. This religious framework is called covenant theology. John Cotton placed his primary focus on the "covenant of grace." "Grace," in a religious context, means that the unmerited favor of God is freely poured upon those who have faith. The "covenant of grace" means that God will freely welcome a person into heaven (salvation) if they profess a belief in Jesus Christ as their savior. On the other hand, some religious scholars felt that salvation was only attainable by a life of good works, known as the "covenant of works." Good works consist of acts performed by a person, such as 1) a belief in Jesus Christ as the son of God, 2) Bible reading, 3) listening to sermons, and 4) praying for the Holy Spirit to come personally to someone. Most mainstream Christian religions teach that salvation is attainable through a combination of grace and good works.

The "Puritan Bible"

Although most sermons had to do with the words in the Bible, it was the interpretation of those words that made the difference from one pulpit to another, as well as from one Protestant sect to another. In the same year that King Henry VIII established the Church of England, Reverend Martin Luther translated the Bible into the German language. Translation into the vernacular horrified many, as they found security and comfort in the more traditional but remote Latin version, known as the Vulgate, that was approved by the Catholic Church. Luther wanted the people of Germany to be able to read it in their homes and understand it. For his translation, he didn't use the Vulgate. He stepped back to its preceding languages, Hebrew, Aramaic, and Greek, and used those for his translation. It was called the Luther Bible, or as it was known in German, the *Lutherbibel*. In England, William Tyndale translated the New Testament into English. Myles Coverdale, who compiled the first authorized edition of the Bible in English known as the Great Bible of 1539, based his work on Tyndale's Bible. The Great Bible was revised again and succeeded by the Geneva Bible. This Bible was completed in different stages, with the New Testament being completed in 1557 and the Old Testament in 1560.

John Calvin was involved in the production of the Geneva Bible, as was John Knox, a Dutch theologian. John Cotton, Anne Hutchinson, and other Puritans used the Geneva Bible, also known as the Puritan Bible. The Geneva Bible showed the influence of John Calvin's religious philosophies because many of the annotations in this version of the Bible were Puritan in nature. The Geneva Bible offended Anglican clerics, who didn't care for its Calvinist flavor. Regardless, it was approved, and it was required by all the churches in Scotland until the Anglican Church received the Bishops' Bible, also known as the Queen's Bible, in 1568 That was later followed by the King James Bible in 1611. That Bible, along with later revisions, is still in use today.

Due to pressures from the Catholic Church and the emergence of diverse religious beliefs during the Protestant Reformation, Queen Elizabeth I created a settlement called the "Elizabethan Religious Settlement" in 1559 in order to maintain uniformity of religious practices. The queen saw to it that the English *Book of Common Prayer* was the catechism for English Protestants. The Geneva Bible and the 1549 edition of the *Book of Common Prayer* were carried over in 1607 to the British North American colonies in their first settlement at Jamestown, Virginia. As a matter of fact, Anne Hutchinson's father was the tutor of John Smith, the explorer and first leader of Jamestown.

Chapter 2 – Her Father's Daughter

The Religious Emigrations

Since its founding in 1534, the Church of England was led by powerful prelates. In 1633, William Laud was appointed to the mighty post of archbishop of Canterbury. It was he alone who determined the flavor and practices of his Anglican flock at that time. When some new movements developed within the umbrella of Anglicanism, Laud went on tirades to obliterate the splinter groups that sprouted from them, designating them as heretical. To a milder degree, Laud subscribed to Arminianism, named after Jacobus Arminius. Arminianism was a branch of Protestantism that was against the belief of predestination promoted by John Calvin, which had accompanied the printing of the Geneva Bible. Although the colonies first started off using the Geneva Bible, the King James Version was considered to be the official Bible by the mid-1600s. Not only did it incorporate the articles within the *Book of Common Prayer*, but it also embraced the structure of a church hierarchy, including its ritual practices, definitions of its theological concepts, and a uniform liturgy as an essential aspect of the religion.

Archbishop Laud wanted all the churches to be absolutely uniform and strictly Anglican in nature, according to his own interpretation. As such, he objected to Puritanism, which was one of the movements within the Anglican Church. Laud was extremely petty when it came to determining whether or not a religious community conformed specifically to those mandates and the doctrinal definitions as they were published in the *Book of Common Prayer*, and he meticulously monitored the churches in England to ascertain their adherence.

Since Laud was vehemently anti-Puritan, he overtly expressed his displeasure if a Puritan-leaning minister failed to scrupulously abide by the Anglican teachings and practices. If any church wasn't conforming to his orders, he could censure the minister, fine him, banish him, or, in some cases, put him in prison. In order to escape the religious persecution by Anglican extremists such as Laud, many of the Puritans planned to move to British America and set up their churches according to their own beliefs. Although John Smith had played an important role in the establishment of the first successful colony in the New World in Jamestown, Virginia, he also discovered a promising territory in the northern region, which he called "New England." The first wave of emigrants to this rugged area settled in Plymouth in the Massachusetts Bay Colony, which was at the time called Plymouth Colony, in 1620. These people were known as the Pilgrims, and religiously, these people were Puritans, that is, people who wanted to "purify" the beliefs and practices of Anglicanism. The Puritans were critics of the new Protestant beliefs that they felt merely mirrored those of Catholicism. Those who were called Pilgrims were even more extreme. They were referred to as "non-conforming" Anglicans and officially separated themselves from the Anglican Church.

In 1629, King Charles I of England dismissed Parliament and ruled on his own. He was very much an Anglican, and his wife, Henrietta Maria of France, was a Catholic. This marriage increased the power of Archbishop Laud and helped put a Roman Catholic slant on church services. At that point, the Puritans were far less comfortable than before. As a result, more English settlers embarked on the arduous journey across the Atlantic Ocean to the territories around Boston, Massachusetts. Primarily, they pursued religious freedom, but they also wanted to look for economic opportunities in the new land. It was a huge territory encompassing lands around modern-day Boston, Salem, Providence in Rhode Island, Connecticut, and New Hampshire.

In 1629, the population of the Massachusetts Bay Colony was a mixture of people under the reformed theological tradition and was mostly Calvinistic in nature. The direction and precepts of each individual church followed the teaching styles of the ministers leading each church but still fell under the umbrella of Anglicanism. More flexibility was permitted in the New World, and the people were free to apply to a church whose practices and ministers appealed to them. Once people were engaging in independent thought, they continued to develop their understanding of religious matters through clergy who were engaged by a church as its teachers.

Unlike many of the clerics of the day, Reverend John Cotton had attended three colleges, Trinity College, Cambridge University, and Emmanuel College. Like Anne Hutchinson's father, he believed in the need for education. Cotton once said, "Who dares to teach must never cease to learn." He despised the elaborate protocols attached to saying Mass and eschewed the wearing of fancy vestments like the surplice. He dismissed them as being prideful and devoid of religious meaning. In addition, he simplified his manner of saying Mass.

The Anglican authorities became enraged at his rejection of those practices. The context of his teachings on revelation and the covenant of grace likewise came to the attention of William Laud, the archbishop of Canterbury. Laud called Cotton definitively anti-Anglican, and Cotton was threatened with possible imprisonment. Consequently, he was forced into hiding and could no longer preach. Now deprived of following his vocation, he emigrated to the New World in 1633, and he was amongst the second wave of emigrants to New England.

Upon his arrival in the Massachusetts Bay Colony, which was officially established under that name in 1628, John Cotton was appointed as the teacher for the First Church of Boston under Reverend John Wilson. Wilson made frequent trips to England, and Cotton used to fill in for him. Cotton's services were extremely well-attended. He believed in preaching plainly and not given into flowery rhetoric, as he wanted both the well-educated and those who came from simple backgrounds to understand the word of God. His love of the Gospels was very obvious, and his sermons were alive with meaning and relevance.

Cotton saw his role within the church as very important, considering the politics and current events of the day. As such, he prepared his sermons carefully. They weren't negatively slanted, as he understood the challenges that his flock faced in life. John Cotton focused upon the relevance of the scripture and its application to the world in which people lived. He became deeply distressed by what he felt was the deviation of religion from the words of the scripture and the abuse of the pulpit to promote a personal agenda. He also disagreed with the Anglican interpretation that there was an absolutely causal relationship between the performance of moral obligations ("good works") and salvation. He emphasized that the grace of God was freely given. Cotton was also a firm believer in the "indwelling" of the spirit, in which each person would be given the means to achieve salvation. Anne Hutchinson particularly related to Cotton, as he was a practical person but glowed with spirituality and wasn't given to the ostentatious frills that sometimes distanced the people from the clergy who served them.

The Great Griffin

Anne and William Hutchinson's favorite clergyman was John Cotton. They had attended his services when he was at the English port of Boston near their hometown. When Cotton departed England, Anne and her husband were distressed because they favored his approach to Puritan doctrine. Anne, in particular, was a fervent Puritan and realized that she also needed to travel to Massachusetts to avoid religious persecution and, additionally, to escape the Black Plague, which was raging through Europe at that time. The Hutchinsons were very concerned about that because they had twelve children, two of whom had already died of the plague.

Anne adopted herbal remedies to prevent the plague, as did many other British people. Many of the British made masks with "beaks" on them and filled them with chopped up dried flowers, mashed wild onions, mint, and crushed minerals. It was their version of natural medicine.

Anne was devoutly religious. Like Reverend Cotton, she believed that God freely imparted his grace upon those who had faith—that is, the covenant of grace. She also believed in divine revelation and held the belief that God could and would impart insights to people individually outside of the Bible. Despite the fact that she wasn't formally schooled in theology, she learned such information from her father, who attended Christ College in Cambridge. From him and from his extensive library, Anne developed an understanding of theological principles. Anne Hutchinson was quite brilliant herself and easily grasped even the most advanced concepts.

Anne was pregnant when Cotton left England, so in 1633, she sent her oldest son, twenty-year-old Edward, on the *Griffin*, a double-masted clipper ship. It was actually the same ship that carried John Cotton. Anne, along with their children, had plans to reunite with their son as soon as her husband could make financial arrangements and wind up his business in London. His fabric business in Great Britain had been prosperous, and his reputation was bolstered by the fact that he came from a prominent family in Lincolnshire, which was the province where he grew up.

In 1634, when she was 34 years old, Anne and the rest of her family set sail aboard the same ship that John Cotton had taken the prior year, the *Griffin*. While aboard, she had a long discussion with Reverend Zechariah Symmes, in which she spoke extensively about her beliefs about God's gift of grace. She also met with a number of women and told them that they themselves could get answers from God through private inspiration, rather than always having to depend upon their ministers. Shortly after their arrival, the Hutchinsons settled in Boston. She and William aspired to become congregants at the First Church of Boston—the church at which John Cotton was a teacher. Most of the churches then had senior pastors, deacons, and teachers. The senior pastors were ordained clergy, as were the teachers. John Cotton was extremely popular in Boston, as he had a gentle way about him and was good at relating to people.

There was a specific procedure for admittance to an Anglican church. Prospective members were questioned about orthodoxy and their related beliefs to see if they conformed to Anglican standards. William was accepted after his first meeting with the church elders, but Anne's admittance was delayed due to her unique views about grace and inspiration. Her views were the same as those of John Cotton, but she was a woman who didn't fit the stereotype, and that alone gave rise to questions. In addition, it was rare to be presented with a woman who seemed to be so knowledgeable about theology. The issue first arose when Anne discussed her views with an English minister, Zechariah Symmes, a hard-core traditionalist of the Puritan persuasion who also sailed to Massachusetts on the *Griffin*. In those days, the ministers discussed new applicants who contemplated joining the Massachusetts Bay Colony. After further questioning, Anne was admitted to the church, though many nursed reservations about her.

Anne and William Hutchinson lived in a two-story home on a small lot on the Shawmut Peninsula (modern-day downtown Boston), which juts into the Charles River. She and William had a large family, and the colony was thirsty for new inhabitants. They needed manpower to tame this raw, new, unpredictable land. Shawmut Peninsula was an idyllic setting for the family. Anne was very active in the community. She had a great deal of experience with children, and she became a midwife for other women in Boston, while her husband was in the city proper engaging in his mercantile trade. Her familiarity with herbs was an asset as she tended to the pregnant women in the community. It was said she assisted well over twenty women in childbirth. Women in those days had many children throughout the course of their life, perhaps as many as twenty.

As part of the requirements to join the Massachusetts Bay Colony, William Hutchinson had to take the Freeman's Oath, in which he swore that he was a "free man," that is, not an indentured servant. Among its terms, the oath required that new colonists pledge allegiance to the British Crown, which was headed up by the appointed governor of the colony, and that they were members of a duly-recognized church. The privileges extended to the signatories of the oath included the right to hold public office, and so, William served as a town deputy and as a selectman the following year. A selectman was someone who was on the executive board of the colonial government. Because women were considered to be subservient, they didn't hold public office but were expected to follow the lead of their husbands and weren't required to take such oaths.

The establishment of a productive civilization had now become the goal for those living in the New World, as it had entered an era when survival was extremely important. Thus, it became more desirable to tap all members of a community, including the women, so that the American experiment would work. So, the importance of the role of women in society became a threat to many men, who were already being confronted with having to contend with an untested country. Men tended to protest when females expressed themselves openly in society because they looked upon women as more competition. Enlightened men were open to the contributions of women, but this adaptation was difficult for many who preferred the status quo. Men sometimes felt that women weren't intelligent enough to comprehend more complex or sophisticated concepts and needed "protection." Protecting the less physically strong is natural to the paternal figures of any species. However, with that came the inevitability of intellectual snobbery. Everyone, women included, fear the harsh reality of losing control. Back then, though, it was the men who feared this loss. To control the reputation of their families, some men felt they had an inalienable right to mandate the behavior and curb the speech of women, particularly that of their wives and daughters.

Acceptance or rejection of a new settler, whether they were male or female, was a highly sensitive point for the founding fathers of the Massachusetts Bay Colony, like John Winthrop. He arrived in Massachusetts in 1630 to escape the rages of religious crackdowns heralded by Archbishop Laud. John Winthrop treated Massachusetts like a foster child and examined the rosters of newly arriving ships to assess the new entries into the colony and expel undesirables. Winthrop also wanted political control and ruled on the governing board of the colony for most of the time he lived there.

Anne Hutchinson's reputation had preceded her, and John Winthrop, who was overly cautious about new inhabitants, had heard about her sharp tongue and mental acuity. He didn't directly address that issue in 1634 when she arrived, though, as he was competing with Thomas Dudley and John Haynes for total control of the colony. These two men were wealthy and knowledgeable in how to administer effectively and wanted the governorship of the colony for themselves.

Although Winthrop was the first governor, Haynes and Dudley served under him as magistrates. In their positions, they exhausted a great deal of time arguing points of governance related to taxation, voting, aspects of the original colonial charter, the judiciary, and eventually became involved in analyzing the nature of the religious beliefs of the newcomers in town like Anne Hutchinson. After having spoken to her, Winthrop felt that "she was a woman of haughty and fierce carriage, a nimble wit and active spirit, a very voluble tongue." In many ways, Anne Hutchinson's personality and, indeed, her life mirrored that of her father. She was her father's daughter.

Chapter 3 – Religion and Rivalries in a Raw Land

Political Problems

Henry Vane the "Younger" came over to Massachusetts with John Winthrop the Younger, the aforementioned John Winthrop's son, and Reverend Hugh Peter, a preacher and a political advisor. Vane was elected as the governor of the Massachusetts Bay Colony in 1636, succeeding John Haynes. Both William and Anne Hutchinson were supportive of the new governor because he was an advocate of religious tolerance, something that was lacking in England. Vane was an active member of John Cotton's church in Boston and was a man ahead of his times in terms of his persistent adherence to the non-conforming Puritan values. His religious viewpoints lay closest to those of Anne Hutchinson, who was his vocal supporter. Cotton recommended Vane also, as he was an independent thinker during an age that encouraged conformity. Historians think of him as a gifted administrator and politician. Because of his intelligence and cleverness, he was seen as a threat by those who preferred utter conformity to the adherence of religious laws. Politically, there was friction among his magistrates, John Winthrop (who used to be the governor) and Thomas Dudley over the set-up of the judicial court. Vane mediated the issue, and they arrived at a compromise.

Pequot War

Although the Pequot War didn't impact Anne's life tremendously, the animosity between the Native Americans and the colonists did not improve with time, as one will notice later when discussing the events of Anne's death. Thus, it is important that this war is briefly talked about.

The southwest area of the Massachusetts Bay Colony adjoined northeastern Connecticut and southern Rhode Island. Offshore lay Block Island, which was isolated from the mainland. The Niantics, who inhabited Block Island, which they called "Manisses," was a tribe that spoke Algonquin. Over time, the Niantics split into two factions, the Western Niantics, who would join with the Pequots in the upcoming war, and the Eastern Niantics, who would ally with the Narragansetts. The Narragansetts, another Algonquin-speaking tribe, shared Rhode Island with other tribes as well as the English colonists under Roger Williams. Even though relations between the tribes and the English settlers were usually amicable, sometimes violent conflicts erupted. Back in 1634, the Western Niantics murdered an English trader, John Stone, by the Connecticut River over a dispute about fishing rights. Despite the deed being done by a different tribe, the Pequots, who controlled much of Connecticut, were blamed. No action was taken against the Pequots at that time, particularly since the people didn't care for Stone, but the colonists became very wary of them.

In 1636, toward the end of Governor Vane's term as governor, the body of John Oldham, an English trader, was found on his ship. From all appearances, he had been slaughtered by natives. Governor Vane then called upon Colonel John Endicott to rally his militia in Massachusetts to prepare to exact revenge upon the troublesome Pequots. Alarmed, Roger Williams, the leader of Rhode Island, immediately contacted Vane, telling him that the crime was most likely committed by the Narragansetts, not the Pequots. Disregarding Williams, Vane sent Endicott ahead to Block Island to invade it, as he was concerned about incursions from the indigenous people on their farms and villages. He also commanded an invasion of the Pequot territory in southeastern Connecticut. To prevent any spread of hostilities, Roger Williams was able to convince the Narragansetts to break their ties with the Pequots and go to war against them as well. Even the Mohegans, who once formed a single faction with the Pequots, joined the fight against the Pequots. Hutchinson and her followers were vehemently opposed to this escalation of violence.

The Pequots fought courageously despite the fact that they didn't possess firearms. They were experts at strategy and knew the terrain well, using it to their advantage. Many English soldiers lost their lives in the early stages of the war. In 1637, the Pequots attacked an English village at Wethersfield, Connecticut, and mercilessly slaughtered men, women, and children. Then the Pequots moved to northeastern Connecticut, along the seashore near today's town of Mystic, where they had a large village. Soldiers from Connecticut under Colonel John Mason rushed into the village and set all the structures on fire. As the Native American warriors tried to escape, they were killed by the Narragansetts and Mohegans waiting outside. Stragglers and survivors from this massacre retreated southward to Fairfield, Connecticut. They were pursued by the English, and the fighting went on until nearly all of the Pequots had died.

The Conventicles

While the Pequot War was going on, the deeply religious Hutchinson held weekly religious meetings, called "conventicles," in her house. Conventicles weren't unusual in England, and the practice continued following the years after the Protestant Reformation until 1648. At the conventicles, the attendees discussed the sermons they heard at the church services as well as the scriptures from which they were drawn. Anne was a gifted and charismatic teacher. It was written by an unnamed woman that she "was wonderfully endowed with the indescribable quality known as magnetism." Thus, her gatherings became very popular, and she developed a following. Several years later, Anne held the meetings more often. Even Governor Vane used to attend the conventicles when he was in office. Most of the members of the meetings were female, but sometimes men even attended, often merchants and seamen. The less structured and informal setting of these sessions interested them, and they were free to openly discuss economic and practical issues and reflect on the ethics they engaged in when conducting business. Because of their business schedules, many of these men weren't available for Sunday services, so the conventicles were opportunities for them to tend to matters of the spirit. There, they discussed the minister's sermons, the Bible, and the covenant theology that Anne espoused.

Conventicles were common in the religious communities of England, and the practice was carried along to America. They not only served the purpose of fortifying religious beliefs but had social functions as well. Colonial women in America were often confined to their homes on weekdays in order to raise their children and take care of the house, excluding trips going to the market. Therefore, they appreciated the company of other adults.

When the men of the area heard about these meetings, more husbands began accompanying their wives. In fact, Hutchinson's audiences swelled in numbers to sixty or seventy, and she began having two sessions per week. As word circulated, a minister of Newton, Massachusetts, named Thomas Weld, noted that "some of the magistrates, some gentlemen, some scholars and men of learning" attended the meeting. Weld felt that the spread of the conventicle movement might make the clergy lose control of their congregations, as they wouldn't be the ones guiding the people in the "right" interpretation of doctrinal beliefs and practices. Therefore, Weld grew suspicious of Hutchinson and portrayed her as being a "conspirator" of sorts, intent on infecting the community with her "venom." In fact, Weld looked upon any woman who led a community such as Hutchinson did as "having stepped out of her place" as a woman. Furthermore, he felt she was being devious and was "a dangerous instrument of the devil raised up by Satan to raise up among us divisions and contentions to take away the hearts and affection for one another."

Puritan Attitudes toward Women

Some of those who lived in the 16th and 17th centuries in America believed that each person was composed of an immortal male half and a mortal female half. The woman in a marriage was perceived to be equal to the man, but the woman was still the "weaker sex" who needed protection. Women weren't permitted to vote or attend civic meetings, not only because of their perceived lack of intelligence but because of an inherent "weakness in their brain fibers." Men preferred they use their time to keep their homes running smoothly and raising children. Contrary to popular belief, women could own property and sign contracts, mostly related to their own property. In some households, husbands asked their wives if they could act on their behalf if they weren't able to be present. It was clear that many men came to realize that their wives were astute, and many sought their advice, although they kept it a secret from other men for fear of ridicule. Some, like Anne Hutchinson, held private power, the power to educate the young and the power to lead other women in religious pursuits.

Puritan women were sometimes seen as potential "Jezebels," not because of some inherent wickedness but because of their powers of persuasion. If they operated outside of the specified female parameters of wife, lover, and mother, they could be seen as seductive. Many sociologists indicate that a female miscreant in colonial times was seen as worse than Eve being tempted by the snake in the Garden of Eden. Instead, she was thought of as the snake itself.

Other sociologists claim that Puritan men had great respect for women. They write that although the Puritans firmly believed in the distinction of the roles of the sexes, women were more than capable of scholarship. This wasn't a commonly held belief, however, and many women were relegated to expressing their thoughts, philosophies, and insights through the medium of letter writing.

Anne Hutchinson observed the fear and anxiety within the Puritan community because of the harshness of their rules. It was recorded by historians that one day, "a woman of Boston…took her little child and threw it into the well and then came into the house and said now she was sure she would be damned because she drowned her child." It was an irrational solution, but it demonstrated the extreme stress many felt because they could never measure up to the insurmountable goals the clergy placed on them. Women, in particular, were made to live in fear and terror of the authorities in New England because religious behavior and civic behavior operated together. Patriarchal inflexibility was traumatic for many of the female congregants. There are historical anecdotes of women who were penalized for infractions of parental obedience, such as in the case of Sara Scott, who was presented in front of the colonial enforcers for "reviling and striking her mother…for undutiful abusive and reviling speeches and carriages to her natural mother." As written in Nathaniel Hawthorne's *The Scarlet Letter*, women who were accused of being adulteresses (whether true or untrue) were made to walk about the town with the scarlet letter "A" sewn upon their outer clothing. This punishment was more common in the colonies later on, and although this penalty was mostly reserved for women, even men had to submit themselves to the same humiliation. For the most part, however, it was as if the male-dominated society in New England feared a female coup d'état. A descendant of Anne Hutchinson, Eve LaPlante, indicated that Hutchinson was derided by one of the Massachusetts governors as an "instrument of Satan," "an enemy of the chosen people," and "an American Jezebel."

Tensions Arise

Before Anne and William Hutchinson became well known in the colony, John Wilson was the senior pastor at the First Church of Boston. Wilson had arrived in Massachusetts along with the earlier emigrants, including John Winthrop, and he was a powerful minister who forcefully emphasized the need for good works in order to achieve salvation. He was away when Anne and her husband first attended the Boston Church, so the congregation became accustomed to their gentle teacher, John Cotton, who promoted the covenant of grace primarily. When Wilson returned, however, Hutchinson and the members of the congregation found Wilson's approach disagreeable. Wilson imparted his message in an authoritarian and strict manner, and his speaking style stood in stark contrast to that of the mild-mannered speech Cotton used.

Wilson's message was also far different from the viewpoints that Hutchinson expressed at her conventicles.

During the course of his homilies, some congregants used to interrupt Wilson and try to initiate theological arguments. Although there were traditional question periods held after the sermons, the orthodox faithful were just expected to ask for elaborations or clarifications of the content of the sermons. The ministers were unaccustomed to being questioned about the religious basis for their sermons. Anne herself was horrified that Wilson would stress that good works were needed to attain salvation and approached Wilson about it. On one occasion, Hutchinson herself actually walked out of Wilson's church, followed by many other women. While leaving during a church service wasn't forbidden, this was an enormous exit of women. Men usually attributed such exits by women as being caused by their "infirmities," but that group was too large to be ignored.

Without a blush, Anne Hutchinson took Wilson's messages home and contradicted him at her weekly conventicles. She was a zealous firebrand and went so far as to say that Wilson lacked the "seal of the spirit," a direct reference to divine inspiration where the Holy Spirit speaks to his elect. The Holy Spirit was seen as a facet of God himself.

In 1636, Anne's brother-in-law, John Wheelwright, also came to Massachusetts. He was an Anglican minister who preached at a church in South Boston. Like Anne, he agreed with John Cotton's theological stance that grace was freely given by God and didn't have to be "earned" through a life of good works. Wheelwright, like many of the non-conforming Puritans, focused upon the covenant of grace, stressing the fact that God gives his grace freely to those who seek it.

Although they had come to the New World in search of religious freedom, some clergymen started repeating the criticisms once levied at the Anglicans in England by Archbishop Laud. Hence, a number of the Anglican ministers in the environs began to question the orthodoxy of John Wheelwright, John Cotton, and Anne Hutchinson. Word raced through the ministerial community about their preaching, comparing it to the prescribed precepts in the *Book of Common Prayer* and reformed theology.

Reverend Thomas Shepard, a scholarly expert, was notified about the deviancy of this group of leaders in the Massachusetts Bay Colony. Having studied at Emmanuel College at Cambridge University and then becoming a minister of the highly respected First Church in Cambridge, a minister at Harvard University, and an instructor of clerics in New England, Thomas Shepard was considered a theological expert of renown. When he heard that these preachers promoted the covenant of grace almost exclusively, he and more local ministers became alarmed. They felt that Anglicanism was becoming polluted with these non-conformist schools of thought, which seemed to be more extreme than their own non-conforming views. They were particularly incensed that Anne Hutchinson—a woman—was bold enough to participate in theological debates, such as the ones she had with Reverend Wilson. Another minister, Reverend Hugh Peter from Salem, said Anne "had better been a husband than a wife; and a preacher than a hearer, and a magistrate than a subject." The tenor of Hugh Peter's response was no longer directed at the content of her messages but rather at her as a person. Not only that, but the fact that Reverend Peter brought up the term "magistrate" had political ramifications as well. After all, in the British American colonies, men—and only men—were permitted to be magistrates.

In the Puritan world of the Massachusetts Bay Colony, the line between civil power and religious power was blurred. In the Massachusetts Bay Colony, the designated religion was Anglicanism, and it was assumed that the people in the colony would support their governors and magistrates along with their religious beliefs. Reverend Peter, in fact, was involved in the civil administration of Salem, where he preached. Like many of the other ministers in Massachusetts, he adhered to strictly orthodox precepts, like those espoused by the archbishop of Canterbury back in England.

One of the local ministers, Peter Bulkley, was a very stiff Puritan minister who had differed with many of the prelates in England because he believed that the ornamental "frills" many of the Anglican ministers displayed in their church vestments resembled that of the Catholics. In fact, he refused to wear the surplice or utilize the ornamental embellishments that the papists and the traditional Anglicans wore. He also taught the covenant of grace, giving it the same weight as the covenant of works. For those reasons, he was called a "non-conformist" and had sometimes run into conflict with the infamous Archbishop Laud in England. However, in many ways, he displayed the same rigidity as the English archbishop and that displayed by Reverend Thomas Shepard because he was horrified that a woman would express herself so openly about religious issues. As one might be able to tell, the issue of Anne was evolving past religious differences; it was instead becoming an issue about women holding a more powerful role in society.

Chapter 4 – Controversies Abound

The Free Grace Controversy

Because of their many sermons about the covenant of grace, John Wheelwright and John Cotton became known as the "free grace advocates." Anne Hutchinson was a "free grace advocate" because she taught the same approach as Wheelwright and Cotton. John Winthrop gave a public voice to this controversy between the covenant of grace ("free grace") and the covenant of works. Politically, Winthrop saw the popularity of John Cotton and his ilk as a threat to his own influence, saying, "In the six months following John Cotton's admission to membership…diverse profane and notorious evil persons came and were accepted into the bosom of the (Boston) church." Then theological tirades began to be shouted from the pulpits Sunday after Sunday from church to church, so Winthrop decided to intervene.

Some reformed theologians felt that teaching about "free grace" would lead to the heresy of Antinomianism. The term "Antinomianism" was coined by Martin Luther during the 15th century, a view that Luther called heretical. The derivation of "Antinomianism" comes from two Greek words meaning "against the law," indicating that one could still be Christian without adhering to moral or church laws. Luther advised that a person did not need to be so overly concerned about keeping the law that they lose sight of the Christian motivation behind the deed they performed. He later felt that would lead to a misconception, so he clarified the issue. Luther admitted that he had been extreme in the beginning by the use of "excessive rhetoric against the law."

The free grace theological movement started during the 1st century but developed during the Protestant Reformation in the early 16th century. People who believed in this movement posited that eternal life is a free gift given by God, demonstrated by the death and resurrection of Jesus Christ on the cross. They believed that the gift of grace is freely given to those who believe that Christ is the Son of God. In other words, faith alone gives a person eternal life.

The Puritan church leaders saw this belief, taken alone and at face value, as a tool for creating passive Christians, who may not necessarily go to heaven without doing good works. Anne Hutchinson was raised as a Calvinist, as were most of the other Puritans. John Calvin promoted the concept of "predestination," which he interpreted as meaning that God has foreknowledge of all events that happen to individuals. Calvin believed not only in free grace but also in the fact that those who truly have faith will persevere throughout their lives in doing good works since faith and good works are intimately bound. However, some non-Calvinistic clergy members misunderstood the concept, perceiving it as being an assertion that God has decided who shall go to heaven and who shall go to hell and that this godly decision was irreversible. Others explained that those who were condemned to eternal damnation were never "true believers" in the first place.

In the religious sense, a "covenant" means a promise made between God and his people. In the case of Adam and Eve, humans broke the covenant. Upon the salvation of Christ, a new covenant was made. In the 17th century, the Puritans went two steps further with the establishment of a social covenant and the establishment of a church covenant.

The "social covenant" referred to the obligation of fellow Puritans to see to it that their families and neighbors kept the law and performed good works. This wasn't an effort to harass others but was rather an attempt to keep society as pure and holy as possible and to unify all within the community. It was believed that keeping the social covenant would facilitate predestination (or prove to others that one was destined for eternal salvation).

The "church covenant" referred to the obligation of attending church and church functions, studying the scriptural texts, and carefully listening to the homilies.

When Anne Hutchinson was conducting her conventicles, she stressed free grace, as did John Wheelwright and John Cotton. They rejected the notion that those who practiced good works and obeyed the law are saved by that alone. They believed it was by faith that one was saved and that the grace of God was freely given. Free grace allowed for the presence of flaws within the human being. A person cannot take pride in deserving eternal salvation, no matter how many good works they did, because all men are flawed. There is no checklist for the number of good works a person has to do.

As a result of their discussions, the group of ministers was satisfied with John Cotton's responses about the covenant of grace and the covenant of works, so they saw no reason to question him further. However, they were still somewhat uncomfortable about Wheelwright's position, and they urged him not to put too much weight upon the covenant of grace but rather to emphasize good works through obedience to the law. John Wheelwright, at least temporarily, agreed with the position of the more powerful clerics in Massachusetts. They next instructed Anne about the role of good works and obedience to the law, saying that both are needed to attain "justification," that is, eternal salvation. Anne claimed, however, that it was through grace alone that one was saved. Good works and adherence to the law, she indicated, are performed for the glory of God, not as a means of attaining salvation.

The ministers were horrified by that and accused Hutchinson of subscribing to "Antinomianism," the aforementioned heretical viewpoint that good works and the law were unnecessary for salvation. That wasn't what she said, but they were convinced that this untrained woman was teaching heresy to the people of the Massachusetts Bay Colony. She was also accused of being a "Familist," which was a 16th-century Dutch belief in the freedom of religion within a community.

The Antinomian Controversy

As mentioned above, the word "Antinomian" is derived from Greek words, and it means "against the law." The term frequently came into the religious jargon during the early days of the Protestant Reformation. However, during the later 16th century, the term Antinomian assumed different shades of meaning.

Antinomians were people who felt they were not obligated to abide by the tenets of a uniform religious code of law. They are saved, that is, they are "justified" by faith alone, without any moral obligation to do good works. Reformed theologians believed that faith would create obedience to the law and ecclesiastical regulations espoused through their congregations. The reformed tradition indicated that faith and good works were both essential in order to obtain salvation. Antinomians believed that the divine indwelling of the Holy Spirit of God spurred righteous behavior on the part of the believer. This state of freedom from the law resulted from the fact that a Christian was "reborn" in Christ, and the Antinomians cited the biblical passage in Romans 7:6, "But now we have been delivered from the law, having died to what we were held by, so that we should serve in the newness of the Spirit and not in the oldness of the letter." Prior to the coining of the term "Antinomianism," the early Christians such as Augustine of Hippo in the 5th century stated, "Love God; do what you will; you won't sin." He saw the integral relationship between the love of God and good works as something that did not need to be spelled out in the law. His view and that of the free grace advocates was the "spirit of the law" rather than the "letter of the law."

The Antinomian Controversy arose following the comments made by one of Martin Luther's students in 1525, and people erroneously began to equate licentiousness with Antinomianism. Anne Hutchinson and the free grace advocates, like John Cotton, became linked with Antinomianism around 1636 shortly after their arrival in Massachusetts. During those days, Christians were scrupulously observant, and it was practically a grievous sin if one didn't adhere to the proscribed beliefs they heard in their church. In most reformed sects, the term was a devastating accusation of heresy.

John Winthrop and the other ministers who took the credit for having founded the colony of Massachusetts Bay were threatened by what they perceived as distortions of their religious beliefs. Although they weren't theologians themselves, they wanted the colonists to strictly adhere to what they said. It was a subtle means of control. Any deviation, however slight, from the pronouncements of the governor and his magistrates was seen as divisive. It could result in banishment from Christian society. Critics of Antinomianism were convinced that any suggestion of it would create chaos within the community, with the more ignorant, barbaric heathens rushing around their communities committing crimes. They reasoned that if there was no legitimate secular or religious authority that people needed to follow in order to reach salvation, there would be no reason to behave morally.

Anne didn't believe that, but more recent commentators leap to the conclusion that she did. It is an easy mistake to make. People of the 17th century were oversensitive to anyone who seemed to stray from the word-for-word interpretations presented from the Sunday pulpits. The real weakness of Antinomianism is the fact that it is too ambiguous a concept. Those who do not examine it thoroughly would understandably leap to the conclusion that Antinomianism totally rejects moral law. It doesn't. Instead, Antinomians rejected the role of good works *alone* in achieving eternal salvation. Many of the Puritans of the 16th and 17th centuries believed exclusively in the necessity of performing good works, and so, Antinomianism was one of the most hated and feared philosophies. The Puritans indicated that there was no way to determine whether people were justified or "saved" except by demonstrating it through obedience to religious law by being willing to "work out their salvation with fear and trembling," according to the words of the scriptures and the Gospels. The "law" they spoke of was derived from the scriptures as interpreted by the clergy and the intellectual fathers of their faith.

The Antinomians of the 17th century, like Anne Hutchinson, were very liberal in hurling the term "crypto-papist" at their contemporaries, an insult to those who believed in the reformed traditions as it meant that they were Roman Catholics at heart. They accused many Puritan clergy members and scholars of being primarily "legalists." In the 17th century, accomplished theologians with international reputations such as Thomas Shepard, who questioned Anne Hutchinson, realized that the issue was far more complex than had at first been anticipated. They taught that men were by nature depraved and that they needed to earn their way into the good graces of God. According to Reverend Thomas Shepard, "…you do not only deserve, but are under the sentence of death and curse of God, immediately after the least hair's breadth swerving from the law by the smallest sin and accidental infirmity."

Even Peter Bulkley, the well-known minister and writer, had been attacked by Archbishop Laud back in England for his non-conformist attitudes toward Anglicanism. Bulkley wrote the book called the *Gospel Covenant* for his followers and forcefully said that the covenant of grace brings salvation. He said, "We are saved by grace, and not by works." He had noted the arrogance and pride of those within the colony who boasted about their good works, and he reacted negatively to their pompous behavior. In the end, Bulkley didn't forcefully support Hutchinson, but that appears now to be more of a case of self-preservation than belief.

In colonial times in Massachusetts, it was important that a preacher keep his reputation in good standing. Hence, ministers, like Peter Bulkley, who could have supported Anne, didn't do so. The people who ran the colony were intolerant of theological viewpoints that appeared to differ even slightly from their own. In effect, they repeated the very behavior that drove them out of England.

Those who failed to parrot the religious viewpoints of the favored clerics risked being forcibly ejected from the colony. In the untamed territories of New England, that was dangerous. However, those who permitted themselves to be vulnerable became strong. Anne Hutchinson wasn't going to compromise her convictions because they were questioned. That wasn't the way of her father before her, and it wasn't her way either, regardless of her gender or status.

Hutchinson's Unique Interpretation

The Puritans who were trained in Calvinism were taught to believe in "predestination," which means that God plans from the very beginning of a person's life whether he or she is to be "saved," that is, go to heaven, or be condemned to hell. Hutchinson rejected that interpretation, at least when presented in that form. She believed and taught that a person could be saved through faith and God's grace, which was freely given. The person then had God dwelling within them. She downplayed the role of good works to an extreme degree. People, Anne believed, would engage in good works to purify the world around them and spread the goodness of God.

Anne also didn't find it necessary to refer to the scriptures by regurgitating what they said; she believed God himself made divine revelations to a person privately within their own soul. It was said that Anne had a revelation of her own while aboard the ship that took her to Massachusetts, as she was able to predict the exact date of her arrival. According to Anne, focusing on one's own personal inspirations eliminates the necessity of scrupulously adhering to sets of regulations and laws. Her viewpoint reduced self-doubt and worry about whether or not a person measured up to moral expectations as expounded by God's earthly ministers. For her, goodness flowed from the grace of God through a person, which would then be reflected in a good life.

The difficulty posed by her views lay in the implication that the law in and of itself was useless to those with true faith. One of the other pitfalls of such an approach lay in the fact that some viewed it as being self-centered, as there was no external evidence that one was, indeed, truly an outstanding moral person. After all, there was no proof that the revelations and inspirations that one might receive were really from God, and there was no evidence that one's behavior was in accordance with moral law. Another pitfall that resulted from this controversy was the fact that this antipathy toward the law opened up the temptation for some to criticize those clergy who taught the covenant of good works.

Reverend Thomas Weld was of the opinion that anyone who taught anything that resembled Antinomianism was motivated by a "spirit of pride, insolence, contempt of authority, division and sedition." He and other members of the clergy felt that Antinomianism was an epidemic that could place the future of the Massachusetts Bay Colony at risk.

Anti-Hutchinson Campaign in Formation

Magistrate John Winthrop went on a campaign to rid Massachusetts of people such as Wheelwright and Hutchinson, as well as the more liberal governor Henry Vane, by accusing them of being Antinomians. Winthrop saw the Antinomian Controversy as a means by which he could eject those who disagreed with his political and theological approaches. As a matter of fact, he spearheaded the passage of a law forbidding residency to new settlers whose beliefs didn't coincide closely with his own. He said that the colony had the right "to refuse to receive such whose dispositions suit not ours." If the people walked in lock-step with his own theological beliefs, Winthrop could continue to hold power over the colony.

Winthrop labeled the Antinomian belief as dangerous heresy, as did many of the Protestant reformists, including the Anglicans. While it's difficult to conclude that Winthrop's political ambitions outweighed his theological positions, it is certain he saw Anne

Hutchinson as a woman who would "split" the colony. There was no tolerance for female activism there.

Justification and Sanctification

Justification, according to Christians, was God's removal of the guilt of sin and the release of the soul from what was called the "original sin," which was originally committed by Adam and Eve when they chose not to listen to God and took a bite of the forbidden fruit. The first stain is washed away in baptism, but justification must be reinforced through nurturing one's continued faith in Christ. That way, a person is considered "saved," that is, they will go into a state of heavenly bliss upon death. While on earth, their good actions are holy as long as they are done through faith. Those acts are, therefore, sanctified, meaning they are "made holy." Sanctification can further be explained as the restoration to the holy image people held before the fall of Adam and Eve.

Anne Hutchinson and John Wheelwright indicated that people did not need to look in their own lives for evidence of one's election to those of the faithful, the saved, and the justified. The opposition, however, felt that wasn't the case. They indicated that one needed to look at their own lives to see evidence of one's justification by comparing their own lives with the words of the Gospel. Those who criticized Antinomianism insisted that the law (religious law) bound all believers, and they felt that the Antinomians denied the usefulness of the law. Antinomians asserted that they didn't need to appeal to the Gospels to know what is right; they simply needed to listen to the "spirit within."

As mentioned before, some of the more traditional reformed traditions like Anglicanism put the proverbial "carriage before the horse," so to speak, by teaching that the kind of grace that engenders faith could only be achieved by the performance of good acts. That way, a person can have their acts sanctified, be justified, and earn salvation.

Anne Hutchinson's approach was more positive. The only way one could lose the grace that God freely gave was to reject it. The unfortunate choice of rejecting that grace could result in a failure to be saved.

The Anglicans and more traditional reformed sects taught that this grace, which brings about justification and salvation, must first be earned. Hence, church members who were judged to be deviating from the religious law must make reparations and beg to be readmitted into the body of the faithful.

The Covenant of Works and Preparationism

This concept was based upon the belief that people who were "reborn" or who "convert" to a belief in Jesus Christ needed to "prepare" for such a life change by performing a series of spiritual steps. Many of the Puritan ministers in the Massachusetts Bay Colony promulgated the view that there was a cause-effect relationship between good works and grace. They further taught that a period of preparation was essential in order to be "born again in Christ" and be made ready to receive the gift of grace from God. In other words, people had to "work" for it, or grace wouldn't be given. Reverend Thomas Shepard, in particular, looked upon himself and other men as being defiled, unclean, and totally unworthy of God by nature. He believed in and taught the vital importance of preparation in order to receive the infusion of the Holy Spirit into one's heart and soul. Others believed that good works were an outgrowth of faith and a consequence of grace.

The difficulty of "Preparationism," as it was defined by some in the Puritan world, was the fact that this period of preparation was totally directed by the minister and the way he interpreted the Bible and religious laws. That approach shifted the control of salvation to the minister—a human agent—and away from God as manifest in the Holy Spirit.

The Covenant of Grace

The Puritans furthermore believed that the people of their faith were redeemed from their innate imperfections through God's divine favor. In other words, humankind could attain heaven if they were "reborn" in Jesus Christ and kept their faith in him. They believed, as the Bible said, "Sin shall not be your master because you are not under the law, but under grace" (Romans 6:14). Anne Hutchinson believed that salvation was attained through faith alone. Reformed theologians, for the most part, taught that the gift of grace was unconditional. Many of the Puritans in New England diverted from that viewpoint by making the performance of works and the keeping of the law a prerequisite for grace.

The strictest of the Puritan churches were like unyielding systems of checks and balances. In the Puritan churches, a pastor would preach, a teacher would see to it that the teachings adhered to the doctrine of the church, the elders would see to it that there were rules to guide the congregants, and the deacons would manage the day-to-day tasks of making everything flow smoothly—that is, financially and practically. Lastly, the churches would see to it that their congregants obeyed.

The Puritans had enforcers within their communities who punished people for breaking some of the most minor rules. Putting people in the pillory or flogging them for slight infractions was a common practice. Women, in particular, had to be careful, as there were many regulations against them, such as making one's opinion known or speaking out of turn. They also needed to keep their children well controlled. If they failed in that, mothers were penalized and humiliated. Colonial punishments could even be sadistic and violent. One could have their ears cut off for eavesdropping or their tongues pierced with hot irons for lying. Banishment from a colony was often used to prevent enlightened ideas from being promulgated. Some of the Puritan communities even forbade a special celebration of Christmas! In one of the newspapers in Boston, it said, "The observation of Christmas having been deemed a sacrilege, the exchanging of gifts and greetings, the dressing in fine clothing (is forbidden). Feasting and similar celebrations are hereby forbidden." There was even a monetary penalty for any infractions of this ordinance, and people were encouraged to report offenders to the authorities.

However, there were differences among the churches. Some of the ministers forbade their people from partying or dancing, while others didn't. Puritans could drink wine and alcoholic beverages but never to excess.

The Massachusetts Bay Colony eschewed change. Gifted leaders with new ideas were seen as too challenging to the status quo and the fail-safe predictability of everyday life.

The Covenant of Works vs. The Covenant of Grace

John Cotton disagreed with prioritizing the covenant of works above the covenant of grace. Many New England ministers preached that the covenant of works was synonymous with legalism and ascribed to it. John Cotton, on the other hand, referred to it with disdain.

Anne Hutchinson agreed with Cotton and, furthermore, realized that guilt was non-productive and deleterious to growth within a community. The precepts hollered from the pulpits of many a dark and somber church frightened the women of Boston in particular, and they felt as if they were under the constant shadow of eternal damnation.

The belief that good works culminate in salvation was appealing to many because people had control over their behavior. If they performed good works, they could then claim they were God's chosen people because they were godly, which could be seen by their actions. The covenant of grace was seen as more passive because no one could "earn" their salvation following that belief.

The Puritan oligarchy either believed in or relied upon the outward evidence of holiness, as would be seen in the observation of the covenant of works. The women, though, were expected to do the opposite—to appear nearly invisible to the male community and be demurely devout.

Anne Hutchinson, John Cotton, John Wheelwright, and Peter Bulkley were concerned about the exaggerated reliance upon good deeds to bring about salvation. It sowed fear, doubt, and even despair among the people of New England. One could get bound up in logistical concerns like counting up one's good deeds to see if one had performed enough of them to qualify as a good person.

Familism

Familism was a branch of religious belief in which the "family of God," or the "family of love," outweighed the personal preferences of an individual member, and all members were equal regardless of religious persuasion or gender. Many Familists were anticlerical and tended to reject the patriarchal domination of the church. Because of the belief in the covenant of grace, the responsibility of salvation was placed upon the individual, with the role of the male clergy being minimized. Reverend Thomas Shepard, in particular, indicated that familism was popular among the "community of women." Clerics like him in the male-dominated church felt that well-intentioned women might discuss matters of religion, but they still needed to consult with the male clergy so as not to be led astray. Both Anne Hutchinson and John Wheelwright espoused an individual's freedom of belief. What's more, it was believed by many in the colony that Hutchinson's conventicles were almost like a cult.

The religious philosophies of the Antinomians and the Familists differed from each other. That is because Antinomians felt that the moral law didn't apply to them, while the Familists felt it only applied to the members of the group or family. Regardless of the differences between those views and that of the free grace advocates, the clerical establishment believed that Hutchinson was an Antinomian and possibly even a Familist. The Familists of the 16th century believed that the community should take priority over the acceptance of a prescribed set of religious doctrines. In other words, Familists were inclusive rather than exclusive.

Banishment of John Wheelwright

In January 1637, John Winthrop called for a day of fasting and praying in order to resolve the divisiveness within the colony created by the discussions of Antinomianism. He wanted to remind the people that he had met with these "free grace" advocates and was protecting the community from any compromise of the religious principles that motivated them to come to the New World in the first place. To reinforce the importance of the issue for the everyday citizen, Hutchinson's brother-in-law, John Wheelwright, was invited to give a sermon. The sermon was later called the "Fast-Day Sermon." He preached the doctrine of free grace and often used offensive imagery, such as "firebrands" and "swords," which—it was said—was atypical language for interpreting biblical passages. It was customary that ministers condemn those who were immoral, but Wheelwright made it quite clear that he rejected those who prioritized the covenant of works over that of grace, as those "sort of people who are to be condemned" and "do set themselves against Jesus Christ: such are the greatest enemies to the state that can be." The language he used was quite inflammatory, and he had occasionally used the term "antichrist" to refer to those who held different opinions. His homily was cited as disrupting the peace within the colony.

Because this was a colony that mixed religion with governance, charges were filed against Wheelwright for sedition. In March of that year, the court convened to discuss his case. It became an issue between those who promoted the covenant of grace and those who promulgated the covenant of works. The court then leaped to the conclusion that Wheelwright's emphasis on the covenant of grace meant that he rejected the emphasis that the orthodox ministers placed on the covenant of good works. Although Wheelwright denied he had rejected their approach, they insisted that it was his intention to reject the orthodoxy of the church. Wheelwright was a fiery minister at any rate, and it is on the court record that he said, "We must lay upon them [the anti-Puritan orthodox ministers] and we must kill them with words of the Lord." The court then found Wheelwright guilty of sedition and contempt of civil authority. When the verdict was read to the populace, there was consternation among the community over the loss of their minister. He had many supporters within the community who were critical of the nearly tyrannical attitude of the ministers in the colony.

Afterward, Governor Vane read a petition in favor of Wheelwright to the people. It said that Wheelwright wasn't guilty of any sedition and that he was like the Apostle Paul because he forcefully opposed those whom he saw as being unchristian. The petition nearly set off a riot because Wheelwright's forceful speaking style tended to pit people against each other. Wheelwright had lost his support, and—by association—so did Hutchinson and Governor Vane, for that matter. Most preferred the status quo.

Wheelwright was banished from the Massachusetts Bay Colony, and the authorities, who feared a revolt, were called into court and questioned thoroughly. John Coggeshall, one of the founders of Massachusetts and a supporter of Hutchinson, did not sign the petition. Regardless, he was questioned. Later on, he was dismissed from his post as the town deputy and banished. Another supporter who spoke up for him, William Coddington, didn't sign the petition. Even though he was a known advocate for Hutchinson and Wheelwright, he wasn't banished, most likely because he was one of the wealthiest men in the colony. If Wheelwright's supporters didn't recant their testimony regarding their support for him and his theological position, they were ordered to surrender "all such guns, pistols, swords, powder, shot and match as they shall be owners of, or have in their custody, under the pain of ten pounds for every default."

One of the predominant factors that influenced the outcome of the court verdict was the fact that Wheelwright was Hutchinson's brother-in-law. It is a reasonable assumption that it was his connection to Anne Hutchinson that may have drawn attention to his sermon. The condemnation of Wheelwright, a relative of hers, was deleterious to Hutchinson, and her gender also helped place her under the shadow of suspicion.

The Political Implications

Anne Hutchinson's meteoric rise and her enduring charisma appealed to Governor Vane. He wholeheartedly supported her, and the legalistic Winthrop couldn't gain a foothold with the population. Other than encouraging the meeting of the clerics with Hutchinson, Wheelwright, and Cotton in 1636, Winthrop couldn't make a move against Hutchinson as long as Vane was the governor and remained popular. Winthrop craved the governorship of the Massachusetts Bay Colony once again. He had been governor before but wanted to be elected again. In order to influence the outcome of the election, he manipulated and conspired to have the election moved from Boston, where Vane was popular, to Newtown (currently Cambridge), where the majority of the population were legalists. "Legalists" refers to clerics and congregants who obsessively adhered to the exact interpretations of Puritan and Anglican beliefs when it came to the law as elucidated by scholars. Legalists believed that the diligent practice of religious law would assure people of salvation. Legalists also emphasized the covenant of works and gave mere lip service to one's dependence upon faith for salvation, that is, the covenant of grace.

In addition to the fact that the voters in the Newtown area would be more predisposed to vote for Winthrop, an election held there would also cause an inconvenience to Boston voters because they would have to cross the Charles River in order to access voting sites. As expected, there were fewer Bostonians who voted in the election, and John Winthrop became governor in 1637.

Henry Vane moved to Providence Plantations, Rhode Island, a colony founded by Roger Williams, another Puritan minister. Williams was sometimes seen as being a Familist because he felt that members shouldn't have to depend upon the state to dictate the moral principles by which they should live. Instead, religious sects needed to care for their own people in terms of upholding moral behavior among their members. He, therefore, believed in the separation between the church and state. Vane didn't entirely favor the separation of church and state as espoused by Williams and eventually became uncomfortable there. He then decided to give up his American experiment and moved back to England.

Chapter 5 – The Hutchinson Trial

The free grace advocates who held public office under the former Governor Henry Vane were voted out during the course of the election cycle. All eyes now focused upon the true source of their discontent—Anne Hutchinson.

On November 7th, 1637, she was asked to appear before the court, which was being held in Newtown, Winthrop's new base. It was a four-mile trip. Winter had come early that year, so the weather was frigid, but Anne and her family made their way there, despite the freezing temperature. Because horses could break their legs on ice, the Hutchinsons had to make their way on land after crossing the Charles River. Anne's son Edward was specifically required to attend because he had signed the petition supporting John Wheelwright prior to his trial and banishment. Four of William and Anne's male children were now of age and, as freemen, were entitled to vote at the trial, so they were in attendance as well.

The trial took place in a cramped colonial meetinghouse. Windows spanned only one side of the room, but deep plunging shadows draped over all the walls. There was no fireplace there, and the low-ceiling room was merely lit by waning candles, giving it an ominous appearance. Anne wore a black dress of serge, a type of twill fabric, and had wrapped herself in a cloak against the chilly wind that occasionally whistled through the cracks of the walls. As was customary, she had a white neckerchief on her shoulders and the traditional coif. Forty magistrates filed into this building, which was known as the Great and General Court of Massachusetts. The court staff alone was large. There were nine magistrates, thirty-one deputies, a whole team of assistants, and fourteen freemen representing the towns in the colony.

The court was deliberately stacked against Hutchinson, as Winthrop had dismissed the judges who were known to favor her. Among the magistrates, called "divines," were Reverend Zechariah Symmes, with whom Anne had carried on a contentious discussion on the ship over to America, and Reverend John Wilson, the pastor in Boston whom Anne had criticized at her conventicle meetings. Reverend Peter Bulkley was one of the most prominent attendees there, as he was admired for his extensive knowledge in the field of theology, but he was known to be very critical of women. Reverend Thomas Dudley, who had been a former governor of the colony, was a known legalist, and he was appointed to serve as the deputy judge. The men of the court wore thick greatcoats, leather gloves and hats, linen shirts, knickers, and thick stockings. They took their places on a long bench facing the people in the court. With a flourish, Governor John Winthrop marched in and took his place in the center. He was to serve as both judge and prosecutor.

Although the court was stacked against Anne, the audience contained many people who supported her. Her husband, William, of course, was there, along with many of his colleagues in the mercantile business. There were traders, merchants, sailors, and brokers—in other words, there were many respected businessmen from the community and those who came from all walks of life. Many of them had, in fact, attended Anne's conventicles.

Winthrop called out officiously, "Mistress Hutchinson!" A cheer went up from the crowd, after which Winthrop impatiently slammed down his gavel. "Miss Hutchinson," he called out again. From the back of the room, she rose and took her place in the center of the room, where the accused was required to stand for the entire proceeding. "Mistress Hutchinson," he continued, "You are called here as one of those that have troubled the peace of the commonwealth and the churches here. You have been known to be a woman that has a great share in the promoting and divulging of those opinions that are causes of this trouble, and...you have spoken diverse things as we have been informed is very prejudicial to the churches and ministers thereof." Winthrop wanted to fortify his position of power by eliminating any infighting or disagreement on religious issues because he felt he would be seen as weak.

To that diatribe, Hutchinson responded straightforwardly, "I have been called here to answer you, but hear no things laid to my charge...what have I said or done?"

Winthrop responded that he had already told her of some of the charges levied against her, but it is clear from the above dialogue that he hadn't. He didn't produce any compelling charges or evidence and seemed to be saying no more than the fact that he and some of the other clerics and congregants simply didn't like what they thought she had said. His entire presentation was based on hearsay evidence and what they had heard by way of gossip. Hutchinson had never written anything down related to the content of her theological beliefs, nor had she presented her opinions in public, other than at her conventicles.

The governor attempted to implicate her guilt by association. She had supported John Wheelwright, who was banished by the community for his fiery sermon, and Winthrop attempted to infer that she was a "co-conspirator" in the "sedition" that Wheelwright was convicted of. Then Winthrop asked why she had supported him and others of the same mind. To this, Anne boldly proclaimed her freedom of choice. "That is a matter of conscience, sir," she replied. Anne firmly believed that the law should be interpreted according to his or her own conscience rather than precisely as the ministers would tell the people. Everyone in the room fell silent, as she was stating one of their dearest principles and using that as grounds for defense—the sacredness of one's individual conscience.

The Conventicle Issue

The deputy judge, Thomas Dudley, then stepped in and brought up the topic of the conventicles she held in her home. He went on to say that the general assembly in the city considered such meetings neither tolerable nor "comely in the sight of God, nor fitting for your sex." Although conventicles were permissible in private, once the size of the meetings became too large, it was understood that a religious representative would come in to approve and monitor them. At that point, they were considered to be "public." However, Anne was unaware of that.

In 17th-century New England, words were considered to be of the utmost importance. According to Puritan thinking, words carried special power but also danger. Although the weight of their words was vital, men—not women—were given full freedom to give any word of advice, cast a vote, and pronounce a verdict in any court or civil assembly as long as it was spoken courteously. The men urged women to "govern" their tongues, and the clerics even quoted the psalmist who said, "take heed that thou not sin with the tongue." Women were admonished to always use "godly speech."

Hutchinson's conventicles were meetings where its members— mostly women—discussed aspects of the weekly sermon and the Bible. However, no member of Winthrop's court had ever attended one of them. The only man with influence who attended her conventicles was Governor Henry Vane. Although the clerics were welcome to attend, they felt that they didn't need such meetings as they had far more religious education than Anne or the attendees. Leaping up, Winthrop forcefully said, "You show not in all this by what authority you take upon yourself to be such a public instructor."

The court then questioned Anne as to why she would teach women at her meetings. She responded with a biblical passage from the Epistle of Titus, "Elder women should instruct the younger." Winthrop then boldly responded with a quote from the First Epistle of Timothy, "I permit not a woman to teach, but to be in silence." Both Winthrop and Hutchinson proceeded to rebut each other by using passages from the Bible. Barb for barb, both the Trinity College graduate Winthrop and the home-schooled Hutchinson were evenly matched.

Anne Hutchinson did believe that women in a private group had the right to discuss and even argue theological principles. She eschewed the viewpoint of the men who wanted women to remain silent about such issues, and she felt that such discussion groups were appropriate marketplaces for ideas. Conventicles had not only been permissible in Christian communities, but it had also been encouraged, and there was no gender preference stated for such meetings. Therefore, it was difficult for the court to contradict this point.

Another problem that the court addressed regarding Hutchinson's conventicles was the fact that she placed tremendous emphasis on the covenant of grace.

The Covenant Issue

Deputy Judge Thomas Dudley questioned Hutchinson regarding her opinions on the traditional teachings of the ministers, which indicated that salvation was won through good works. That specific issue was taken up in a question-and-answer dialogue:

> Dep. Gov. Thomas Dudley: When they do preach a covenant of works do they preach the truth?
>
> Anne Hutchinson: Yes, Sir. But then they preach a covenant of works for salvation, and that is not truth.

The dialogue above directly addresses the point Anne was trying to make. That is, salvation cannot be attained through the performance of good works; it is freely given through faith. One doesn't have to struggle for one's whole life hoping to earn it because it is freely given from God.

The Authority Issue

Winthrop indicated Anne Hutchinson had broken the Fifth Commandment ("to honor one's father and mother") by disobeying the "fathers" of the British Commonwealth, who were her spiritual parents, by holding these meetings at her home. Winthrop believed that the men in authority were there for the outworking of God's grace, which originated from above.

As her meetings had become so well attended, the court questioned her right to hold such meetings. Anne questioned them mockingly, asking them if her name had to appear in the Bible in order for her to be permitted to do so. "Must I shew my name written within?" she asked. Winthrop also accused her of making disparaging comments about the ministers of the colony. He then went on to say that if she was to say erroneous things, they would officially reprimand her so that she would become a "profitable member" among them, and he reminded her that he and the members of the court were her judges. She said, "You have no power over my body, neither can you do me any harm—for I am in the hands of the eternal Jehovah, my savior."

In hindsight, it is clear that John Winthrop felt threatened by her popularity. Even though it might be said that Governor Winthrop had secular political ambitions, it is also true to a great extent that he felt men who were in authority in the colony were placed there by God to be good rulers to keep peace and unity. He saw this incoming influx of Puritans as weakening a frontier community in an untested New World. The Puritans were so God-fearing that they primarily focused on life after death and might put aside practical considerations for their physical survival in the coastal colony.

Winthrop was sincerely convinced of his own importance within the community and felt that the eminent people within the colony were divinely charged with the religious and civil obligations to hold the community together. Therefore, they had been elected by these God-fearing people to direct their lives in accordance with both religious and secular directives. What Winthrop imagined was that any acceptance of the Hutchinson philosophy would open the gates to a mob of radical anarchists. The English of the 17th century greatly feared a society in which many different viewpoints were tolerated because factions that were too disparate created friction and sometimes even civil wars. The English had been brought up on a "sameness" that dictated, in essence, what everyone believed in: how they behaved and the penalties for deviation. That dedication to uniformity created a peace of sorts because it was a predictable way to live.

In 1630, John Winthrop had a sermon published called *A Model of Christian Charity* in which he warned people that they must follow the direction of their political and religious leaders because their community was "a city upon a hill, and the eyes of all people are upon us." He drew a phrase from the Sermon on the Mount in the Bible, which stated, "You are the light of the world. A city located on a hill cannot be hidden." He then went on to write that if citizens fail to follow the directives of their leadership, God will withdraw his help from them. Anne indicated that she had abided by religious leadership. She was a member of Reverend John Cotton's congregation and supported his approach to understanding justification. Like her, he expressed the belief that God freely gives his grace to the elect, those who were chosen to enjoy eternal bliss. Since Cotton was an influential and eminent member of the community, the court conducting Anne's trial couldn't find any adequate reason to reject her for being among his followers. However, there were other ways to attack her character, and they next discussed the content of her messages.

During the trial and in Anne's presence, the governor addressed some of the ministers about what Anne had said or done that they found offensive. Reverend Hugh Peter spoke up, saying that he had once asked her what difference there was between her John Cotton and him. Then he went on to elaborate: "Briefly, she told me there was a wide and broad difference…He [Cotton] preaches the covenant of grace and you the covenant of works, and that you are not able ministers of the New Testament and know no more than the apostles did before the resurrection of Christ. I then put it to her, 'What do you think of such a brother?' and she answered he 'had not the seal of the spirit.'" Peter and the other ministers were astounded at her response and, not coincidentally, her brutal frankness.

Winthrop was among those shocked at this recollection from Peter. It was Winthrop's firm belief that political power and ecclesiastic authority were inseparable. To monitor the religious beliefs of the residents of the community would result in the control of their political preferences. Thomas Weld, who was active in subduing Hutchinson and the free grace teachers, felt the same way. They wanted full control over the community and didn't want to jeopardize their positions, either religiously or politically. No women had ever challenged them quite so forcefully, but they felt unsure about ejecting her due to her large following in the community. If they could continue the proceedings, they felt as if they might be able to get her to compromise and redeem their image and reputations among her followers.

So, the next day, they addressed the sensitive issue of Anne's so-called "disparaging" remarks about some of the ministers' homilies, particularly the fact that the ministers put much more stress upon the covenant of works than the covenant of grace. Deputy Judge Thomas Dudley claimed that Anne Hutchinson "has depraved all the ministers and has been a cause of what has fallen out." During the aforementioned meeting between Hutchinson, Winthrop, Wheelwright, and Cotton, Hutchinson had been guaranteed that her statements were strictly private, that is to say, "off the record," and she was taken back by this breach of confidence. She went on to say that what she herself believed or what she said in private should not be considered a crime. However, at this trial, the presiding court ignored any prior guarantees of confidentiality, and her words became known publicly.

Once that occurred, Anne demanded that the court ministers swear to the statements they made. All but Thomas Leverett, a lawyer and church elder, Deacon John Coggeshall, and John Cotton were reluctant to do so. Thomas Leverett stated that Anne didn't say the ministers shouldn't teach the covenant of works but that they didn't teach the covenant of grace as clearly as Reverend Cotton did. Deacon Coggeshall's statement indicated that he didn't feel Anne had been as critical as the court contended. The members of the court realized that Coggeshall was a fervent supporter of both the banished John Wheelwright and of Anne Hutchinson, so they paid little heed to his statement. John Cotton ducked the topic by saying that he didn't recall Anne's words exactly, adding that he never heard her teach anything against the ministers with regard to the covenant of works, nor diminish the importance of good works as necessary for salvation. He then shied from giving Anne any appreciation for her having preferred his church to those of others. It was a betrayal in a sense when he said, "I was very sorry that she put comparisons between my ministry and that of others."

John Cotton was one of the clerics questioned by Winthrop in October when the issue first came to a head in 1636. Unlike Anne, he was soft-spoken and conciliatory. Anne was a woman, and John was a man, and that seemed to make all the difference in this case. The central theological matter had to do with the doctrine of free grace, or covenant of grace, which Cotton had been a forceful promoter of. In fact, he was seen by some as having sparked the Antinomian Controversy, which became a bone of contention between the legalistic Puritans and those who believed in the power of grace freely given by God. Cotton, as a mild-mannered and likable man, managed to escape censure during the infamous October meeting held at Winthrop's residence between himself, Wheelwright, and Hutchinson.

With regard to having made some negative statements about Wilson and other ministers, Anne didn't deny the charges levied against her but said that she was reluctant to explain her statements in open court. She relented, however, indicating that the truth bound her to do so. She stated that she felt some of the local ministers did their congregations a disservice by failing to explain the covenant of grace. However, she was somewhat embarrassed at the brashness of her words, which is why she preferred to speak about this in private rather than in open courts.

The Revelation Issue

Anne was extensively questioned because she said that she was led by God in her interpretation of the scriptures and the accompanying inspirations she said she received from God. She said that "I could not open the scripture; he (God) must by his prophetic office open it unto me." Following that, the court assistant and Mr. Dudley carried on another dialogue:

> Mr. Nowell, court assistant: How do you know it was the spirit?
>
> Anne Hutchinson: How did Abraham know that it was God that bid him to offer his son, being a breach of the sixth commandment?
>
> Dep. Gov. Dudley: By an immediate voice?
>
> Anne Hutchinson: So to me by an immediate revelation.
>
> Dep. Gov. Dudley: How! An immediate revelation!

Governor Winthrop and the other deputies objected to Hutchinson's use of the term "immediate revelation." They feared that she recommended that a type of religious anarchy would prevail in which individuals would become passive in religious observation and act upon their own spiritual impulses, whether they were true or untrue.

The last statement wasn't intended as a question. It was rather an exclamation of disbelief. It was clear by this point that Anne wouldn't be given the benefit of the doubt. Hutchinson continued after that by way of clarification:

> Anne Hutchinson: By the voice of his own spirit to my soul. I will cite another scripture, Jeremiah 46:27-28—out of which

the Lord showed me what he would do for me and the rest of his servants. But after he was pleased to reveal himself to me. Therefore, I desire you to look to it, for you see this scripture fulfilled this day and therefore I desire you that as you tender the Lord and the church and commonwealth to consider and look what you do. You have power over my body but the Lord Jesus has power over my body and soul.

With regard to what she said at her conventicles, Anne stated she felt she received direct inspiration and revelations from God that she was to be saved, along with those who likewise believed in the covenant of grace. Hutchinson stated that she herself was directly inspired by God, stating that her mystical experiences were "inward convictions of the coming of the spirit." Furthermore, she indicated that anyone could communicate directly with God without the assistance of a minister reciting biblical passages or their own prayers. This sentiment ran counter to the Puritan belief that the scriptures should only be interpreted by the church's duly ordained ministers. By saying that she had been directly selected by God to deliver some of God's messages at her conventicles, many concluded that she was blasphemous. Thomas Shepard taught that no one simply hears the voice of the Holy Spirit. It is "heard" through the reading of the Gospels and meditation.

This claim was especially offensive to the colonial and religious authorities. If Anne's attitudes about personal revelations were accepted, then there would be no need for ministers or civil authorities because they were viewed as one and the same. It could result in the "utter subversion of both churches and the civil state," in Winthrop's words. In order to preserve the unity of their orthodox beliefs, the Puritans firmly held that confession of one's faith is the role of the organized church, not the individual.

What's more, personal communication from God through the Holy Spirit might be perceived as a substitute for the words in the Bible. While Hutchinson believed and taught from the words in the Bible, others in the community might feel that they didn't need to refer to the scriptures. In its extreme, it might encourage moral laxity.

Anne said that, through the words of the Bible, "God can communicate directly to one through those words." However, she stretched the concept of revelations by God by indicating that a person could receive a revelation from God *outside* the Bible. This offended the male sensibilities of the ministers, as it threatened their control over people's behavior. They stipulated that it was *their* interpretation of the words of the Bible as pronounced from the pulpits that would help lead the freemen of the Massachusetts Bay Colony to salvation.

Also necessary was a process of rigorous instructional preparation led by church elders, in which they addressed the basic doctrines their churches promulgated and the outward behavior they expected of all colony inhabitants. This became a way in which the Puritan elite could control the people, as they were all required to attend church services and follow the directions of the religious establishment.

Hutchinson collided with the theologians of the times when she said she was "in direct communication with the Godhead" and was "prepared to follow the promptings of the voice within against all the precepts of the Bible, the churches, reason, or the government of Massachusetts." This was disquieting to Puritan ministers and even the men in the community who prided themselves as the protectors of their wives in terms of biblical understanding.

Toward the end of her trial, Hutchinson felt a divine revelation within that pumped her full of courage that was powerful but foolhardy. Without trepidation, she spoke out loudly, announcing, "The Lord gave me to see that those who did not teach the New Covenant had the spirit of Antichrist."

Thomas Dudley questioned John Cotton with regard to that. Although the ministers had questioned Cotton several months prior to this trial, they were somewhat ambivalent about his standing, and

Cotton knew that. So, he became uncomfortable and even a tad annoyed that he was being drawn out on the revelation issue. However, he did admit that there was some rationale for Hutchinson's remarks.

Some of the deputies were hesitant on what to think about Anne, including William Coddington, who said, "I do not see any clear witness against her, and you know it is a rule of the court that no man may be a judge and an accuser too," ending with, "Here is no law of God that she hath broken nor any law of the country that she hath broke, and therefore deserve no censure."

Winthrop, anxious to tie up this ordeal, drove the court to consider a verdict. Putting aside the theological impact of Hutchinson's message, Winthrop considered her revelations, in particular, as seditious and in contempt of the court. "If therefore," he said, "it be the mind of the court, looking at her as the principal cause of all our trouble, that they would now consider what is to be done with her." He then made a move to have Anne Hutchinson banished from the colony.

The Verdict

Some of the court deputies voted against banishment, but the majority of the court members voted in favor of it. There were two phases to Hutchinson's sentencing: her right to remain in the colony and her membership of the church itself. She wasn't allowed to go home, so she was detained under house arrest with Joseph Weld, the brother of Reverend Thomas Weld. Governor Winthrop even had the audacity of referring to her as a "prisoner." Anne became ill during her four-month detention and wasn't allowed to see her family. William, her husband, and some of the older children spent the time scouting out some areas along the coast where they could move.

After her detention, Anne was called back before the court again. Many of Hutchinson's supporters didn't attend the session this time. Some had retreated back to their homes, but there were many who traveled with her family in search of another church and community that would suit their spiritual needs. Even after all of this, Anne still had her faithful following.

Unfortunately, this became a time when the orthodox ministers could have their vengeance on her—vengeance cloaked in the religious garbs of the various major or minor theological points of doctrine. They discussed the issue among themselves, and many of their conversations were nothing more than the "mincing of words." Then they met with Anne at her home church in Boston to go over a list of errors that Anne had committed. It was a nine-hour session, in which she elucidated her thinking on those topics. At the end of this very grueling session, they managed to zero in on two "dangerous" errors – that the Holy Spirit dwells in a justified person, and that no sanctification can be used as evidence of justification, that is, that they had been saved. The other so-called errors were merely listed. Most of them were basically opinions that arose from the ministers without a foundation in Anne's testimony. Anne was approached privately by many of the ministers who wanted to discuss the issues, compose retractions, and reform her teachings. In March 1638, Hutchinson read some retractions. Some had to do with her highly contended views of the sermons of the legalistically inclined ministers, what she said about sanctification and justification, and her prophecy about the demise of the colony.

Toward the end of the session, John Cotton made a double-handed statement. He said, "I would speak it to God's glory that you have been an instrument of doing some good amongst us...he hath given you a sharp apprehension, a ready utterance and ability to express yourself in the cause of God." He then made some references to the notion that she believed in the Antinomian philosophies and then betrayed her in the cruelest of terms by saying her opinions "fret like gangrene and spread like leprosy, and infect far and near, and will eat out the very bowels of religion."

Cotton's soft approval of Anne's actions might have possibly satisfied the ministers until Reverend Thomas Shepard, who had called her "very dangerous" even before hearing all of the evidence of the case, let out a tirade in which he called her a "Notorious Imposter" and a "Heinous Liar." Reverend Joseph Wilson, the first pastor Anne criticized, jumped into the verbal foray and stated the final sentence on March 22nd, 1638:

> Forasmuch as you, Mrs. Hutchinson, have highly transgressed and offended... and troubled the Church with your errors and have drawn away many a poor soul, and have upheld your revelations; and forasmuch as you have made a lie...Therefore, in the name of our Lord Jesus Christ...I do cast you out and...deliver you up to Satan...and account you from this time forth to be a heathen and a Publican...I command you in the name of Christ Jesus and of this Church as a leper to withdraw yourself out of the Congregation.

Although she wasn't required to speak in her own defense, Hutchinson did so. She leveled a shriveling retort intended as a prediction, uttering loudly, "You liked to put the Lord Jesus Christ from you, and if you go on in this course you will bring a curse upon you and your posterity, and the mouth of the Lord has spoken it."

Governor John Winthrop then said, "I am persuaded that the revelation she brings forth is delusion."

Her dire prediction regarding the fate of the colony was incongruous to her typical nature. Although she didn't prevail at the trial, her defense was brilliant. However, one might come to the conclusion that her spirit was broken by the overwhelming trauma of the experience.

Whatever the case might have been, that last statement of hers was tantamount to blasphemy. Whether those words were spoken by an arrogant woman who had deluded herself into believing she was a prophetess or the cry of a weary soul that felt abandoned by the Holy Spirit within her, one shall never know.

Chapter 6 – After the Trial

Anne Hutchinson was 47 years old when her trial concluded. In addition, she was pregnant and in frail condition, so Weld housed her for about a month until new arrangements could be made. While there, she was visited by Reverend Hugh Peter and Reverend Thomas Shepard on a number of occasions to attempt to persuade her to recant her "errors." They had hoped that her sentence could be lifted and felt that her admission would justify their actions.

As happened in the case against John Wheelwright, Hutchinson's supporters were given a choice to recant. Those who didn't were told to surrender their pistols, powder, and ammunition. There were 75 men from whom weapons were confiscated.

Two of Anne Hutchinson's supporters, William Coddington and John Clarke, along with William Hutchinson and a few courageous followers, came together and embarked on a torturous journey toward current-day Rhode Island. They had heard about a preacher named Roger Williams, who had literally been chased from territory to territory in Massachusetts because of his religious views. He eventually ended up in Rhode Island and was trying to establish a new church settlement there.

Anne Hutchinson in Rhode Island

Roger Williams was a Puritan who came to New England back in 1631—just a few years earlier than Anne. In some ways, he was a man ahead of his times. He had seen the negativity generated by state-run religions and was looking toward providing people with more liberty to choose their faith. In Europe, there were already burgeoning religious sects that were distinctly different in their beliefs, and Williams wanted to avoid conflict among any new settlers over the freedom to practice their religion. Such conflict constantly interfered with the running of state and foreign affairs in other colonies. What's more, it deleteriously affected the economy.

Williams was particularly interested in being a clergyman for the church in Salem, as he had heard they tended to have separatist views and did not want to strictly model the Church of England. The people of Salem invited him there, but the clergy at Boston had heard of his separatist views. As a result, Salem withdrew their invitation.

Plymouth, Massachusetts, which had been founded by the Pilgrims, had declared themselves as being separate from the Church of England, so Williams went there to explore the possibility of coming there in a clerical capacity. He encountered two difficulties with Plymouth: 1) the churches there didn't display much of the separatism from the Church of England that Williams had expected, and 2) Williams discovered that the Pilgrims had just occupied the area without making any recompense to the tribes that lived in the area. He wrote to King James I in that regard, and he also accused the king of a "solemn lie" when the king claimed he was the first monarch to have a colony in the New World. Roger Williams was right; Elizabeth I was the first English monarch to claim the new land, but one wonders why he felt it necessary to bring that uncomfortable point out in the open. Williams was, in some ways, a rebel.

After this, the First Church of Salem invited him to replace the late Reverend Samuel Skelton, despite the earlier protest by leaders in Boston. Williams was well-liked there. In 1635, Salem wanted to expand their territory and applied to the General Court of Massachusetts to take over some land in Marblehead Neck. Of course, Williams' reputation was widespread, and the civil authorities disliked him, claiming he had "dangerous opinions." The Massachusetts Bay Colony was anxious to rid themselves of free thinkers like Roger Williams, so they held up Salem's application for Marblehead in order to seize the opportunity of charging him in General Court on counts of treason and sedition. That was the same technique they used for Hutchinson and Wheelwright just two years later. Like Hutchinson, Williams, too, was banished. Williams weathered many journeys seeking a territory where he and his flock could settle and practice their faith in freedom.

In spring 1636, Williams arrived at an area in Rhode Island ideally suited for his followers, who were mostly planters. The settlement Williams helped them find was located around current-day Providence, Rhode Island. The Narragansett tribe welcomed them there, and Williams himself invited other dissenters from the Massachusetts Bay Colony to join him.

In 1638, William Coddington, John Clarke, and William Hutchinson met with Roger Williams. Although Williams had control of the land, which he bought from the Narragansetts, he was determined to separate religion from the colony's government. Hutchinson's group was pleased with that and formulated the Portsmouth Compact in order to establish their own church. John Coggeshall, who had supported Anne at her trials, was one of the main signatories. Hutchinson's adult male children also signed it, as did her husband, of course. Twenty-three men signed it in all, followed by five more newcomers a few months later. After the initial signing of the Portsmouth Compact, which took place in March 1638, they awaited the arrival of Anne Hutchinson. Roger Williams officially established the Colony of Rhode Island, and his own settlement was called Providence Plantations.

The month of April in 1638 was bitter. Yet Anne was a tough pioneer woman who would never let the weather interfere with her objective, so she walked sixty miles in the snow to get to Rhode Island. Anne was deathly ill from her late-in-life pregnancy by the time of her arrival. Because of her age, the fetus was badly malformed when Anne delivered the baby in May, and it resulted in a "hydatidiform mole," which is a badly malformed stillborn infant. A young minister who had been traveling back to Massachusetts heard about this and described the fetus to Governor Winthrop, saying it looked like "a bunch of transparent grapes." The minister, though, overlooked the fact that Hutchinson nearly died of blood loss during the unfortunate event.

Dissension in Rhode Island

William Coddington then settled the Hutchison group in an area they called Pocasset, currently called Aquidneck Island. However, he wasn't a wise administrator and became too autocratic. In 1639, a citizen of Pocasset, Samuel Gorton, spoke up for the discontented populace. He organized a "civil body politic" that ousted Coddington. The tumult was just limited to the civil government because of the separation of church and state, so, therefore, it never accelerated to theological debates. The matter was handled civilly, and the people of Pocasset elected to change the name of the settlement to Portsmouth. They created a code of laws and created stipulations for a trial by jury. Anne Hutchinson's husband William was elected as its new magistrate.

John Winthrop of Massachusetts kept track of the events in areas near Massachusetts, such as Rhode Island, and was very quick to insult Anne Hutchinson again, along with her husband this time. He wrote about the dissent in Portsmouth, saying,

> The people grew very tumultuous and put out Mr. Coddington and chose Mr. William Hutchinson only, a man of very mild temper and weak parts (weaknesses), and wholly guided by his wife, who had been a beginner of all the former troubles in the country and still continued to breed disturbance.

As a result of the political dissent, Coddington, with his supporters, moved to an adjacent area and called it Newport. His followers included some very strong politicians such as John Coggeshall, who had traveled with Anne from Massachusetts. Other prominent men such as Reverend Nicholas Easton, William Brenton, Jeremy Clarke, and Henry Bull settled in Newport as well. John Winthrop lost no time in insulting Reverend Easton of the newly created Newport when he said, "Other troubles arose in the island by reason of one Nicholas Easton, a tanner, a man very bold, though ignorant."

Within a short period of time, amends were made between the two groups, and Newport united with the Portsmouth group. Coddington, having learned his lesson from the rift, modified his ways and was elected as governor. William Hutchinson agreed to become his assistant. The name of "Newport" was dropped, and the town became known as Portsmouth.

Anne Hutchinson and Roger Williams kept in touch for a while. In fact, Anne's sister, Katherine, married Richard Scott and lived in the Providence settlement. Williams had a civic non-sectarian government there, and a number of people from other denominations—Quakers, French Huguenots, and Jews, among others—lived there as well. Through Roger Williams, Anne Hutchinson formed relationships with the Narragansett tribe there. The women of the tribe often traded goods and furs with the colonists.

Late in 1638, Roger Williams was interested in the Baptist faith but didn't become an official member. John Clarke, who had accompanied William and Anne Hutchinson to Rhode Island, exercised the freedom of religion permitted in Rhode Island and established the First Baptist Church in Newport.

Winthrop Strikes Again

In the time that had passed since the trial, Winthrop continued to be obsessed with the experience he had with Hutchinson and what he may have considered to be a failure in the Puritan experiment in New England. Winthrop was, as a matter of fact, one of the founders of this community, and the Hutchinson trial and its aftermath took its psychological toll on him.

When he heard of the birth of Hutchinson's deformed fetus, Governor John Winthrop lashed out at Anne Hutchinson by sending a missive to Rhode Island. In the cruelest of terms, he said that the unfortunate birth was a punishment from God. As he spoke about his doubts, he was told of a similar incident that took place during the course of Anne Hutchinson's trial.

Anne, who was a midwife, had assisted a member of her conventicle, Mary Dyer, in childbirth. The child's brain didn't develop normally, and the infant died shortly after birth. In the 17th century, unsuccessful births were superstitiously associated with evil or seen as a punishment from God. The mothers were always blamed for them. Once they saw the pitiful condition of the fetus, Anne and her assistant midwife, Mary Hawkins, contacted John Cotton. Cotton rushed over, saw the condition of the fetus, and buried it secretly. Regardless of the fact that Cotton attempted to protect the reputation of the mother, word got out. Winthrop found out about it when people told him the rumor of Mary Dyer's "monstrous birth." In an attempt to justify his actions during the trial of Anne Hutchinson, Winthrop had the body of the baby exhumed and wove a wildly fabricated story about it. In his journal, he wrote that when the body was removed from the grave, women vomited violently and their children had convulsions. In describing the fetus, he wrote:

> It was a Satanic mix of a woman-child, a fish, a beast and a fowl all woven together into one, and without a head. It was much corrupted and holes in the back misshapen as the like had never been heard of. The back parts were on the sides and some scales were found. It was so monstrous and misshapen. The ears were like an ape's and grew upon the shoulders; the nose was hooking upward and the breast and back were full of sharp prickles. The back parts were on the side and, instead of toes, it had three claws with talons like a young foal. Above the belly it had three great holes like

mouths and out of each of them a piece of flesh. It had no forehead, but in its place there were four horns.

Winthrop then stated that Mary Dyer had been an upstanding member of the Puritan community in New England until she came under the influence of Anne Hutchinson. He then blamed that misfortune on Anne Hutchinson, saying that she "brought forth not one, but thirty monstrous births or thereabouts…None of them was of human shape." It seems that the content of a woman's uterus had become a theme for religious debate and hasty judgment.

The Puritans held the odd belief that the soul of a male escaped the body and was resurrected after death to have a heavenly life with the angels in eternity. There was no mention of women, though. Typically, women were seen as temptresses sent to test men's faith by trying to lure them away from salvation.

Anne's husband may not have believed that women were temptresses, but he did believe in life after death. And at the age of 55, his beliefs provided him much comfort, as he passed away in Portsmouth in 1641 when Anne was fifty years old. She felt insecure after that, especially because the Massachusetts Bay Colony was now right on the southwest border and clamoring to expand. She was concerned that they would incorporate the area where she lived at that time.

For her health and well-being, Anne decided to travel to New Netherland with a group of people she had met in Roger Williams' settlement. Her oldest son, Edward, decided to return to the Massachusetts Bay Colony, and he reconciled with the ministerial authorities there. He moved back to the family homestead in Boston and became a lieutenant in the Military Company of Massachusetts. While in Rhode Island, Edward had purchased a tract of land near Providence and held on to it.

New Netherland

New Netherland was a Dutch colonial settlement that encompassed a large segment of today's New York City, the state of New York, and New Jersey. It was established in 1614 and administered by the Dutch West India Company. The principal function of the Dutch West India Company was trade, and they used the Hudson and East Rivers, along with its tributaries, to transport goods from the New World to Europe. Willem Kieft was the director of the Dutch West India Company in 1641 and wanted to possess various large plots of land to expand the colony. Therefore, he negotiated with the Algonquin Native American tribes, also known as the Wappinger Confederacy, who occupied parts of New Jersey, Connecticut, and New York. The deal was laid through a series of smaller contract purchases from this confederacy of Native Americans who dwelled on the coastal lands alongside today's Pelham Park Bay and Eastchester Bay—all of which fed into the Long Island Sound and the Atlantic Ocean.

The Dutch West India Company bought it for axes, beads, and knives, which would have been the equivalent of around four thousand dollars. That figure breaks down to less than two cents per acre. William Kieft was a greedy man who shortchanged the Native Americans for their land. He also simply stole more plots alongside the purchased land.

Dissension between the Dutch and the Native American Tribes

To the Native Americans, the "purchase" of a plot of land by settlers meant that the colonists were allowed to occupy the land, farm it, and build villages and towns. For their part, the tribes believed that they retained the right to use the land seasonally but were expected to respect the property rights of the colonists. The native people of the Americas were nomadic, so that understanding suited their lifestyle well. Thus, they often hunted on colonial farmlands and fished in the waterways of the colony. By virtue of these purchases, the tribes felt they had agreed to share the land with the settlers. Of course, that occasionally produced friction, and there were violent outbursts.

On one occasion, in the summer of 1641, members from the Raritan tribe, an Algonquin-speaking people, were accused of stealing a canoe from a trading vessel and some pigs from David de Vries, whose tobacco farm was located along the Hudson River. Kieft interfered and demanded the return of the canoe and payment for the pigs. As tempers flared up and hostilities were kindled, Kieft dispatched Cornelis van Tienhoven and seventy men to exact payment. As it turned out, the Raritans hadn't stolen the pigs (other colonists had), but they were still blamed for it. Because the Puritans were innocent of stealing the pigs, they paid nothing. The whereabouts of the canoe remained unknown. However, the Dutch soldiers attacked the Raritans anyway and killed several of them. The Raritans then burned de Vries' farm and destroyed his tobacco sheds.

Willem Kieft was inexperienced and unskilled in dealing with the native peoples, and it did not help that he saw them as inferior. When Willem Kieft noted that the native peoples continued to use the waterways for fishing, he took that opportunity to propose that the tribes pay tribute to the colonists who were using the land. A number of Dutch settlers who had lived in the area with the native people in peace for nearly ten years warned against such an arrangement, realizing that it would lead to problems. Kieft ignored their advice and made a proposal to the tribal elders that they could license the use of the area for fishing. It was rejected, as would be expected. Kieft ignored the pleas of some of the Dutch settlers and tried to extort payments nonetheless.

Manhattan, at the time, was cohabited by both the Native Americans and the Dutch settlers. On Manhattan Island, a young Weckquaesgeek lad murdered a Dutchman named Claes Swits, a bartender, as an act of revenge for the murder of the boy's uncle. Kieft and the Dutch authorities demanded that the tribe hand over the teenage Weckquaesgeek boy, but the tribe refused to do so. The issue of revenge arose in New Netherland, but the older settlers still didn't want to stir up the native peoples.

Noting the ambiguity of the colonists to generate hostilities, he appointed a Council of Twelve Men to decide whether the settlers should make war upon the tribes or not. To garner interest in war, Kieft presented the case of poor Claes Swits as an example of the dangers of having Native Americans living among the settlers. After much finagling and persuasion from two of the more powerful members, Kieft was able to convince his Council of Twelve Men to move ahead with a plan to attack the tribal nations in the area.

When Anne Hutchinson arrived there in 1642, she wasn't entirely aware of the growing antipathy of the Native American tribes in the region. The Weckquaesgeeks and Tappans dwelled just north of her home. They were being threatened by the more powerful Mohegans and Mohawks, who were encroaching on their territory. So, to protect themselves, they asked Kieft to aid them. However, he refused. Thus, they fled to southern Manhattan and eastern New Jersey and camped around the area of "Pavonia" and "Communipaw" in current-day Jersey City. Kieft, on the other hand, was on a campaign to rid the entire Dutch settlements of Native Americans. He then rallied his troops to attack them. De Vries, the man whose farm was attacked just a year prior, took pity on the plight of these displaced tribesmen and attempted to draw up a truce.

Neither de Vries nor many of the settlers who had lived peacefully among the Native Americans until Kieft arrived, wanted a war, but Kieft was determined. It was a matter of urgency because the tribal nations along the East Coast, specifically the Lenape, were increasing in number.

Kieft's War and the Death of Anne Hutchinson

At the beginning of 1643, Kieft ordered his troops to preemptively attack the tribes in Pavonia. De Vries described the attack, which was tantamount to a heartless massacre of Native Americans:

Infants were torn from their mother's breasts, and hacked to pieces in the presence of their parents, and pieces thrown into the fire and in the water, and other sucklings, being bound to smallboards, were cut, stuck, and pierced, and miserably massacred in a manner to move a heart of stone. Some were thrown into the river, and when the fathers and mothers endeavored to save them, the soldiers would not let them come on land but made both parents and children drown.

While Kieft's War was being waged in small battles and skirmishes throughout New York, Joseph Sands, a young man related to Anne Hutchinson's husband, agreed to build a fine house in a wooded area, strewn with large rocks that had formed there in the glacial age. They selected an area on higher ground near Split Rock, a huge craggy boulder that is located in today's Pelham Bay, New York, near the city of New Rochelle. Other historians place her original homestead in today's Co-op City, New York. Both cities would have been located in the Bronx, a borough of New York City today. There was a wide but shallow river there along with two creeks nearby, which would have been a good source of water for them, as well as for their crops, chickens, a few head of cattle, and pigs. The river that inundated that plot is called the Hutchinson River today, and it was, of course, named after Anne.

As Joseph Sands was constructing Hutchinson's new home, a collection of Native Americans from the Siwanoy tribe came by, shouting loudly before sitting down. Sands was confused by that but continued to work. After all, the Hutchinson plot lay to the east of acres of woods where the Siwanoy people hunted and fished. The Siwanoys were a part of the Wappinger Confederacy and spoke an Eastern Algonquin language. Hutchinson's settlement was located in this wooded area of Pelham. So, after Anne and her family moved into the dwelling, she and her family were on friendly terms with their Native American neighbors. The Dutch people who lived in the vicinity, however, came to her and explained the hostilities that had already occurred in other places. Anne, though, was unafraid.

The Siwanoy people were among those who fought in Kieft's War. And it did not matter that Pelham was an English settlement and not a Dutch one; the Native Americans drew no distinction between the different settlements.

On August 20th, 1643, Chief Wampage and his group of Siwanoy warriors came up to Anne's house, requesting that she tie up the dogs. Thinking there was nothing unusual about that, she did it. According to Eve LaPlante:

> The Siwanoy seized and scalped Francis Hutchinson, William Collins (her son-in-law), several servants, the two Annes (mother and daughter), and the younger children— William, Katherine, Mary, and Zuriel. One of the Hutchinson's daughters, "seeking to escape," was caught as she was getting over a hedge, and they drew her back again by the hair of the head to the stump of a tree, and there cut off her head with a hatchet.

Then they dragged the bodies of the Hutchinson family into the house and burned it to the ground. One of Anne's daughters, nine-year-old Susanna, wasn't there, as she was off in the woods picking blueberries. Upon her return, she was kidnapped. The warriors admired her for her red hair, and she was taken to their encampment. It was said that Susanna was renamed "Autumn Leaf" and lived with the tribe for anywhere between two to six and a half years. Once Chief Wampage discovered that Anne Hutchinson was famous, he took on the name of Chief "Anhõõke" for Anne Hutchinson, a custom among Native Americans for when one personally kills a well-known figure.

This was a merciless and brutal way for Anne Hutchinson to be torn away from this earthly world, but it also must have been puzzling to her. After all, Anne had spent her life spreading the hope of grace and love to an ungrateful people in an unforgiving land.

Chapter 7 – And What Became Of?

It is interesting to note that only one of the people who featured prominently in Anne Hutchinson's life died because of religion. Geopolitical motivations appear to have freckled the lives of the others after Anne Hutchinson died, and many were caught up in the dark and dirty webs of their own weaving.

Archbishop William Laud

In 1640, the great migration to New England ceased. The people began to focus once more on England because the political scene there promised hope and change. Archbishop Laud, who had been ejecting non-conforming ministers and their followers, merited the wrath of King Charles I by creating too much divisiveness within the Anglican Church by stringently executing that policy and was imprisoned. There was no legal basis for eliminating Laud as a future threat to England, so they levied a charge of treason against him without solid evidence. His trial ended without a verdict, but the king hadn't forgotten a cloaked insult Laud had levied against him when he called Charles "a gracious Prince who knows not how to be great or be made great." King Charles I, with the aid of Parliament, passed a bill of attainder, which would allow for a person to be found guilty without a proper trial. On January 10th, 1645, Laud was beheaded.

John Winthrop

In 1640, John Winthrop was forced out of office as governor because the economy of the Massachusetts Bay Colony suffered a severe setback when a lot of the colonial religious and civic leaders exited along with their followers.

In 1644, a book was released in London called *A Short Story of the Rise, reign and ruin of the Antinomians, Familists & Libertines that infected the Churches of New England* about the Hutchinson trial and its implications. Although the author of the work was never explicitly stated, it is assumed that John Winthrop wrote it. In the book, the author labels the errors of those "heretics" as being the result of a conspiracy primarily promulgated by Anne Hutchinson, who, along with her "fomenters," had attempted to manipulate the clergy and magistrates of the colony. He spoke of the "lamentable death of Mrs. Hutchinson" but retracted any trace of pity for her by calling it a "remarkable judgement of God." The author goes on to explain how the ministers and magistrates of the colony drew attention to the errors of Hutchinson and the Antinomians at her trial, as if somehow warning others that doctrinal deviations would not be tolerated.

Reverend Thomas Weld wrote the preface to that book, in which he spent three and a half pages placing Anne Hutchinson at the center of the controversy, saying that she used "sleights" and "tricks" to influence the people who attended her weekly lectures. Weld used numerous gendered terms to denounce Anne, with remarks that referred to her opinions as "brats," who were "hatched and dandled." He also referred to Hutchinson's miscarriage as a judgment of God, as Winthrop had done before.

An opposing viewpoint to *A Short Story* was expressed by Reverend John Wheelwright from exile in New Hampshire. He indicated that those who were banished from the colony were disenfranchised for what could only be minute "theological lapses." He went on to write that some of the more studious members of the colony stood up to what amounted to the abuse of authority. Wheelwright railed against Winthrop's use of Hutchinson's miscarriage as evidence that she had acted wrongly.

John Winthrop was elected to the governorship once again in 1642, but he was ousted in 1644 after having cost the colony a lot of money by failing to provide military support to a French trader who had been bringing a lot of business into the colony.

While John Winthrop was busy attempting to get reelected, he wasn't taking care of his lands, and they fell into ruin. He then needed to ask people to bail him out financially. He died of natural causes in Boston in 1649.

Reverend John Wheelwright

After his banishment, Wheelwright had been invited to go to New Hampshire. He spent some in the town of Exeter preaching at a church there, then moved to Wells, Maine, where many of his parishioners followed him to a small church. Wheelwright had been deeply distressed by his banishment and wrote several treatises defending his position.

Due to the time it takes for publishing, his treatise, *Mercurius Americanus*, was published in 1645, but his banishment had been lifted the year before, and the court issued a document to that effect, saying that "Mr. Wheelwright has his banishment taken off and is received as a member of the Commonwealth." He went to Hampton, Massachusetts, where he joined Pastor Timothy Dalton.

In 1654, a petition was developed by many of his supporters requesting that Wheelwright not only be permitted back in the colony but also be permanently vindicated. It was received favorably by the court, and Wheelwright was vindicated by the religious authorities in the colony. However, after his experience with banishment and his ambivalent reception back into the community, he became disheartened and returned to England a year later. Since he had been vindicated, though, he was free to continue preaching.

Wheelwright remained in England when Oliver Cromwell was the head of state, and Wheelwright preached in his old home town of Allford, as well as in Belleau. However, after the death of Oliver Cromwell, who usurped and executed King Charles, conditions became difficult for the Puritans, so Wheelwright returned to New England and was installed as a minister in Salisbury, Massachusetts.

In 1677, Wheelwright and one of his church members became embroiled in bitter arguments over several issues regarding the boundaries of Salisbury and a new subdivision of Amesbury, as well as Wheelwright's objection to a Quaker presence in the town. Usually, there weren't disagreements over boundary lines, but Wheelwright's opposition to the wealthy Major Robert Pike reached a fever pitch. Wheelwright appealed to the court, and Pike vociferously objected when the court ruled against him. Soon after, Wheelwright excommunicated Pike. The feud didn't end there; instead, it persisted for months until a special committee of respected people from the congregation were tasked with the job of resolving the dispute peacefully. Even though the strident Wheelwright fanned the flames of hostility, it was agreed that both would accept equal blame and that Pike would be restored as a fully recognized member of the Church. The chroniclers at the time said that this was done in deference to Wheelwright's advanced age of 85. There was no further contention between Pike and Wheelwright after that. When Wheelwright became feebler, he was given an assistant to share his church duties. He died of a stroke in 1679.

Reverend Thomas Weld

Weld was one of the most vociferous ministers who presided over the trial of Anne Hutchinson. In 1641, he and Reverend Hugh Peter, another one of Hutchinson's opponents, tried to ingratiate themselves to Governor Winthrop by offering to alleviate the economic downturn incurred by the colony, which had started a year earlier. He, along with Peter and a businessman by the name of William Hibbens, sailed to England for two purposes: 1) to raise funds for maintaining and expanding Harvard College (later Harvard

University) and 2) to obtain ownership of a portion of current-day Rhode Island to expand the colony and therefore increase its revenue. They were somewhat successful in obtaining donations from the British people for Harvard, but there was a serious legal issue that arose due to their efforts to acquire the Rhode Island territory. Roger Williams, a religious leader who had been banished from Massachusetts, had a rival claim for the same territory based upon an agreement with the Narragansetts who lived there.

In 1643, Weld, in order to bolster his right to lay claim to that land, wrote a fundraising book called *New England's First Fruits*, in which he asserted that he had made inroads into evangelizing the native people of New England and that they were anxious to become members of the colony. To strengthen his claim, Weld sent an agreement called the Narragansett Patent, which was a contract granting British settlers ownership of the land. However, the document he sent turned out to be a total forgery. Roger Williams made a strong case for his side of the issue by discrediting Weld's and Peter's claim, as well as the fabricated information in the book *New England's First Fruits*. Williams was ultimately given the charter for his colony in 1663 and won the right to settle in Rhode Island. Anne Hutchinson was welcomed into his colony, as indicated earlier.

Because of his fraudulent claim, Thomas Weld was charged in the General Court of the Massachusetts Bay Colony, but he ended up staying in England and never showed up for his trial. Even if he had wanted to return, he couldn't because he spent what money he had and became impoverished. Rumor has it that he hid out near London. According to his family records, he died in 1661 or 1662 in England.

Reverend Hugh Peter

Hugh Peter, who was one of Anne Hutchinson's accusers and voted for her banishment, went over to England with Reverend Thomas Weld in 1641 to solicit money for Massachusetts for the expansion of Harvard College and to lay claim to a segment of Rhode Island for the New England colony to expand. Unbeknownst to Peter, Weld stepped over the legal line when he forged a document trying to prove ownership of the land. Peter was, in the meantime, raising money for the upcoming English Civil War in Holland, and he continued to involve himself in the civil war that was brewing between Parliament and King Charles I. Peter sided with Parliament against the king and was assigned to recruit troops and be their chaplain in the upcoming battles. In 1645, he wrote to General Sir Thomas Fairfax, "Sir, one of the greatest comforts I have had in this world next to the grace of God in Christ to my poor soul, has to a member of your army, and a spectator of his presence and you of it." After the war, Oliver Cromwell seized the throne from King Charles I and beheaded him. Hugh Peter participated in that execution himself.

After that, Peter had an eminent position under Cromwell himself, making proposals for legal reforms and similar treatises. Under Cromwell, Peter became a chaplain who accompanied Cromwell's troops when they annexed Ireland and invaded Scotland. Peter spoke with fervor against the Irish, but downplayed his support for Cromwell in Scotland because those people had fought in the earlier phase of the English Civil War and shared a similar religion—Presbyterianism.

Hugh Peter had his wealth of lands and lived a lavish life at the castle at Whitehall, where Cromwell also resided. However, upon Cromwell's death, Peter was ousted from his position by Cromwell's son and successor, Richard. Richard was a weak leader and was soon usurped by the restoration of the Stuart monarchy, which had been sheltered in Scotland. In 1660, in order to gain the good graces of the heir apparent, King Charles II, Peter traveled to St. Albans near London to greet the newly restored king and his military entourage. General George Monck, who led the military escort, ignored him. Every dignitary knew who Peter was, as he had a very distinctive voice. As soon as the royal parade had entered the palace, Hugh Peter was arrested on the charge of regicide. It had been said that

Peter heavily disguised himself and acted as one of the executioners of King Charles I. Peter was sentenced to be hanged, drawn, and quartered—one of the most gruesome and horrible forms of public executions.

Peter left behind two contradictory reputations. Some indicate that he was a jocular man, honest, kind, and a victim of circumstance. Others, though, said he was an adulterer, an embezzler, and a drunk, reeking with cruelty and verbal venom. Peter was maligned as much as Anne Hutchinson was and, like her, suffered a brutal, frightful, and bloody fate.

Mary Dyer

Mary accompanied Anne Hutchinson after Anne was banished in 1638, and—like Anne—was humiliated when Governor Winthrop found out that she had also given birth to a deformed baby who was stillborn. This occurred during the course of Hutchinson's days' long trial. Winthrop blasted Mary's reputation, and people gossiped about it for quite some time. Mary stayed in Rhode Island at the Newport settlement Coddington ran. Her husband, William, was the general recorder for the colony and took Mary with him in 1651 when he went to England on business. After her husband sailed back to New England, Mary stayed behind in England for about six years. History has not recorded why she stayed there. It seems odd because she had six children at home in Rhode Island.

While in England, she came into contact with a religious group of Quakers, which was known at the time as the Society of Friends. The religion appealed to Mary even more than the version of Puritanism taught by Anne Hutchinson, John Wheelwright, and the free grace advocates. The Society of Women actually permitted women to act as ministers and proselytize.

In 1657, Mary Dyer returned to Boston, Massachusetts, now as a Quaker. The Quakers wore a recognizable headscarf, and she was shocked when she was immediately imprisoned. William Dyer rushed over to the jail and bailed her out. He wasn't permitted to allow her to live in Boston, so she had to travel to Weymouth, another town in Massachusetts.

In Boston, and in other parts of New England as time went on, the Puritans were even less tolerant of the Quakers than they were with Anne Hutchinson. They hated the Quakers, especially for their proselytizing efforts, and banished them from the colony. If the Quakers didn't comply, the leaders of the colony dealt out harsh punishments to both men and women, like severe whiplashings in public. For other offenses, they physically tortured them and sometimes even cut their ears off. Anne Hutchinson's younger sister, Katherine Marbury Scott, was also a Quaker and was made to endure ten lashes. She and her husband then moved to Providence, Rhode Island, in 1658. It was said that they were the first Quakers in Roger Williams' Rhode Island.

In the meantime, Mary Dyer and her Quaker associates traveled from Weymouth, Massachusetts, to New Haven, Connecticut, preaching and trying to convert people to Quakerism. The magistrates of many of the Puritan towns in Massachusetts were becoming more alarmed by the increasing numbers of Quakers, and many were imprisoned. In 1659, they passed a new law indicating that they were banished from the Massachusetts Bay Colony "upon pain of death."

Mary Dyer heard that many of her Quaker friends had been incarcerated in Boston and went there to visit. As soon as they arrived, Mary Dyer and the two other Quakers who came with her—both men—were imprisoned. Governor John Endicott brought the men before him, stating,

> We have made many laws and endeavored in several ways to keep you from among us, but neither whipping nor imprisonment, nor cutting off ears, nor banishment upon pain of death will keep you from among us. We desire not your death. Hearken now to your sentence of death.

Then, Governor Endicott brought Mary Dyer before him and said, "Mary Dyer, you shall go from hence to the place from whence you came, and from thence to the place of execution, and be hanged till you are dead." She then bowed her head and said, "The will of the Lord be done."

Her companions were all hung from an elm tree, while Mary waited her turn. She was led up the ladder, and a noose was placed around her neck. Then, suddenly, a reprieve was announced. Her husband and son had been working vigorously for her release, and the General Court had granted the appeal and gave Mary a reprieve on the basis that she was a woman.

Dyer then returned to Rhode Island but continued to be grieved by the deaths of the other Quakers, especially those who hung right before her very eyes. It was a cruel and devilish law that had been written by those who called themselves sanctified and holy. She then considered a way in which she might attempt to force the authorities in Boston to change that law. In 1660, she decided to scapegoat herself and traveled to Boston in deliberate defiance of their ban against Quakers. Ten days after her arrival in Boston, she was brought before Governor Endicott. Her husband desperately tried to secure another reprieve for her, but it was denied. Mary was hanged from the old elm tree on June 1st, 1660.

Reverend John Cotton

Once considered to be Anne Hutchinson's mentor, John Cotton distanced himself from her once she awarded herself the gift of prophecy by the Holy Spirit. Cotton believed that people could find the truth in the scriptures but that they should not separate themselves from the law.

Cotton was opposed to the separatist view held by Roger Williams, so he tried to lure him back into the fold. He also urged Williams to persuade the older sects of Puritanism and the budding religious sects of Quakers, Presbyterians, Baptists, and Anabaptists to rejoin the Church of England and set up self-governing entities while still upholding the basic doctrines of reformed theology. To promote Congregationalism, a system that promotes local churches to be self-governing, he proposed that each church take responsibility for guiding their own congregations and uphold the religious laws approved by them. His best-known work was *The Way of the Churches of Christ in New England,* which was published in 1645. Because it was considered to be too stringent, the book wasn't used as a guide for the churches, but it did become a reference in setting up the legal system in Massachusetts.

In 1651, Cotton became extremely inflexible and conservative. In fact, he turned into a very strict legalist. He condemned those who held some Anabaptist views and permitted public whippings and imprisonment for other deviant views as well. A former clerical friend of his, Richard Saltonstall from England, wrote to him, saying, "It does not a little grieve my spirit to hear what sad things are reported daily of your tyranny and persecutions in New England as that you fine, whip and imprison men for their consciences." Cotton did not change his ways too much before his death. To be fair, though, Cotton died only a year later of pneumonia.

Roger Williams

Anne Hutchinson left the relative safety of Rhode Island after disputes arose over the possession of Rhode Island. After the Pequot War, which took place between 1636 and 1637, and the difficulties over Anne Hutchinson and those whom they called "heretics," the people who lived in Massachusetts and Connecticut allied with each other in an effort to rid the area of the tribes in Rhode Island— namely the Narragansetts and the Mohegans—and simultaneously expel Roger Williams and his settlers from Rhode Island. This military alliance was formed in 1643, after Anne Hutchinson had relocated to New Netherland. After the fictitious claim of Thomas Weld was dismissed, Williams rushed over to England to fortify his demand for a colonial charter of Rhode Island. He wrote a book, *A Key into the Language of America,* to demonstrate his knowledge of the tribal languages and wrote about the richness of their cultures.

One of his objectives was to encourage the English to stop belittling the tribes and respect them as sons and daughters of God. He wrote:

> Boast not proud English, of your birth and blood;
>
> Your brother Indian is by birth as good.
>
> Of one blood God made him, and you all,
>
> As wise, as fair, as strong, as personal.

He also wrote *The Bloudy Tenent of Persecution for Cause of Conscience*, which defended his argument for the separation of church and state. In the text, Williams drew extensively from scriptural quotations. The book was a 17th-century "bestseller," and Williams won the official charter for the colony of Rhode Island just a month before the death of Anne Hutchinson in August of 1643.

Following that publication, Williams wrote a number of books in an effort to convince people that the separation of church and state was the best possible solution to avoid religious persecutions and to free up civic administrations. He said that there was no scriptural mandate for a state-imposed religion. Williams did, however, believe that those portions of the Ten Commandments that constituted moral law should be the basis for civil laws.

Williams never committed to just one religion, although he did lean toward Baptist teachings. At some point between January and March 1683, Williams died, although the causes of his death remain unknown.

Edward Hutchinson

Historians generally agree that Edward Hutchinson accompanied his mother to Rhode Island in 1638. He was one of the founding fathers of their settlement of Pocasset. After serving there for a couple of years, he returned to Boston. Because there were no charges levied against him as a result of Anne's trial, he was permitted to return. Edward was in his twenties at the time.

He took over the family house and made arrangements for its upkeep by hiring caretakers. It is said that he welcomed Anne's daughter, Susanna, home after her release by the Siwanoy tribe, who had kidnapped her when her mother was killed. The approximate date she arrived in Massachusetts was 1647 when she was twelve years old.

Edward saw to it that she was taken care of until she married John Cole in 1651.

Edward was a peacemaker and improved relationships with the government. He was well-liked, personable, and was an active member of the colony militia. In 1653, he was made captain of the artillery. In 1658, he was elected as a court deputy. His cousin, Patience, had married a Quaker, and he was instrumental in campaigning for the tolerance of those who practiced different religions. Up until that time, Massachusetts had been imprisoning Quakers who had emigrated into the colony. They were treated cruelly in captivity, and Edward campaigned against that kind of treatment. In 1668, those who were imprisoned were released.

Edward got along with the native people of Rhode Island fairly well, as they were very peaceful. In fact, the Narragansetts of eastern Rhode Island and the Wampanoags and Pokanokets in the province of Plymouth, Massachusetts, had workable relations with the Pilgrims. The Wampanoags served under their *sachem*, that is, their chief, Wamsutta. He was very fond of calling himself "Alexander." After the death of Wamsutta, his brother, Metacomet, who assumed the English name "Philip," took over and decided to take a more hostile stance, as the colonists were increasing in number, encroaching on their hunting and fishing areas, and becoming embroiled in minor conflicts. The Pilgrims in Plymouth avoided Metacomet, as he was a young and impulsive young man intent on making a name for himself as a hero. Colonists hastily erected garrisons and built defensive walls around their towns in both Rhode Island and eastern Massachusetts. Every able-bodied male was recruited into the militia, including Captain Edward Hutchinson, who was called to active service and given command of a company of men.

Rumors of this pending war with the tribes were leaked to court magistrates by a Native American informer, John Sassamon. Sassamon was a Harvard graduate and a recognized translator and negotiator for the colonies. Not long after he did this, Sassamon was found murdered. In Plymouth, three warriors serving under Metacomet were hauled before the colonial court and questioned. As a result of the trial, the three warriors were hanged in June 1675. Under Muttawmp, the Nipmucs of western and central Massachusetts and the Pennacooks around Massachusetts Bay then joined the Native American alliance.

The hostilities started in Plymouth when several bands of Pokanokets attacked homesteads and slaughtered the inhabitants on the night of a full moon in the summer of 1675. There was also a vicious attack on the major town of Swansea, where buildings were burned or destroyed and several people were killed. Militias in Bristol, Rhode Island, staged a retaliatory strike on a tribal encampment nearby. The war moved to Middleborough, Mendon, Northfield, Deerfield, Hadley, and Brookfield, all towns that were located in Massachusetts.

In Brookfield, Anne Hutchinson's son, Edward, was the captain of an artillery unit. He and Captain Thomas Wheeler fought vigorously to ward off the onslaughts from the Pokanoket and the Nipmuc tribes. Toward the end of the siege at the fort they were stationed in, Wheeler and Hutchinson negotiated with the sachem of the Nipmuck, attempting to pull together a truce. It was unsuccessful, though, and the two of them were ambushed. Edward Hutchinson died of his wounds the following day. His youngest sister, Susanna, and her husband, John Cole, later settled on a Rhode Island land tract owned by Edward.

King Philip's War was not over yet. In Springfield, Massachusetts, along the Connecticut River, moderately sized groups of Native

American fighters attacked the town's grist mill. They destroyed nearly all of the buildings in the town, save for the blockhouse, which is a small two-story building with openings intended for rifles.

In Rhode Island, the faithful Narragansetts weren't involved in the war for the most part, with the exception of Sachem Canonchet and his band (a sachem refers to a paramount chief). The rest of the Narragansetts gave refuge to other tribes, specifically the Wampanoag warriors, along with their families who had been hiding in the Assawompset Swamp, just below Providence, Rhode Island. Despite the fact that the Narragansetts were mostly peaceful, many of the militias from other colonies didn't realize that and attacked them indiscriminately, burning their dwellings. They also attempted to take the fort alongside the Great Swamp, which was frozen at the time. The fort at the Great Swamp, near today's Kingston, Rhode Island, housed thousands of people, including men, women, and children. The indiscriminate attacks by the colonial forces of Connecticut, Massachusetts, and Rhode Island brutally wiped out nearly a thousand unarmed people. Others fled into the bitter cold across the frozen water. Those survivors who managed to make it to Aquidneck Island in Narragansett Bay were taken care of by some kind-hearted colonists.

Mary Rowlandson, the wife of Reverend Joseph Rowlandson, who was one of the survivors of the battle, wrote:

> Now is the dreadful hour that I have often heard of in time of war, as it was the case of others, but now my eyes have seen it. Some in our house were fighting for their lives, others wallowing in their blood, the house on fire over our heads, and the bloody heathen ready to knock us on the head if we stirred out...the bullets flying thick, one went through my side, and the same (as would seem) through the bowels and hand of my dear child in my arms.

The war raged on until 1678, with many dying on all sides. However, there was only one victor of this war, and the colonists were the ones to claim that name. Although, it should be noted that this war only increased tensions between the settlers and the neighboring tribes.

Roger Williams, who was in his seventies, was there in Providence, Rhode Island, during this cruel and bloody war. Providence was nearly in ruins, as were many other cities and towns in Rhode Island due to the warring Narragansetts who didn't remain neutral. In a desperate effort to stop the war that nearly ruined his colony, Williams often shuffled over to the warriors on his weakened legs, begging them to stop. On one particular occasion, he pointed back toward his burning house and said, "This house of mine now burning before my eyes has lodged some thousands of you for these ten years." Later on, Williams lamented to his brother, "I told them they had forgotten they were mankind and ran around the country like wolves tearing the innocent and peaceable. They confessed they were in a strange way."

Conclusion

Rather than being a feminist in the sense of promoting women's rights, Anne Hutchinson demonstrated them. She was intellectually advanced and more than willing to stand up for her beliefs. Not once during her trial did she ever use her gender to solicit sympathy. Hutchinson eschewed the weakness traditionally attributed to women of the 17th century by simply not being weak. She was, in the words of her nemesis, Governor Winthrop, "as bold as a man." While much of what Winthrop said about her wasn't true, that statement definitely was.

Anne Hutchinson was a woman born before her time. The faith she imparted was a faith she lived every day. It gave her the willingness to be vulnerable in the face of adversity, and through her vulnerability came strength. She was cautious, but not to the point that she was about to surrender her convictions to please those who labeled her as a weak or subservient woman—or as someone who bent or broke like a reed in the wind. What's more, she knew who she was and what she stood for. Part of Anne's charm was that she spoke to her followers on their own level. Her language wasn't derived from a process of literal thinking and blind faith like that of other Puritans. She didn't carefully define terms like "sanctification" and "justification," which may have been her own undoing, but she knew she didn't have to. Those terms had already been inculcated in her listeners. Hutchinson instead presented an approach to religion that helped them think for themselves and develop an inner conscience.

The Anne Hutchinson affair served to highlight the main issues that plagued the New England communities, including the danger of conducting a church trial on heresy and bridging that over to indicate sedition, a civic/criminal offense; the influence of a political campaign for governorship on religious beliefs and practices; the disenfranchisement of citizens who disagreed with the religious beliefs of the majority; the right to reject people from settling in the colony without the permission of civil authorities, and; the right to banish people from the colony on the basis of theological differences or controversy.

One of the elements often overlooked by commentators about the controversy between the Puritan elders and Anne Hutchinson is one of political survival. The Puritans came over to New England to preserve their religious beliefs and way of life. However, they were immediately confronted with the harsh and unforgiving environment of a raw new world. The one major element they shared in common was their faith, and they needed that unity to survive. There was no room for heterodoxy in the Puritan world of New England because they weren't ready for it. But some members, such as Anne Hutchinson, were, and they were willing to fight for it.

Perhaps the greatest pitfall that occurred to the Puritans and people of other faiths in the New World was the combination of church and state. In Europe, the most prominent legal structure upon which to model a government was the religious establishment. It had a hierarchy, governing bodies, a set of laws, and a judiciary of sorts. It would be quite a challenge for people who grew up in that world to think of politics that could work outside a religiously flavored framework. One would have to develop a set of rights based upon moral law, the kind of law that could hold an intelligent society of human beings together in peace.

The problem of creating a colony based upon religious affiliations is the fact that its leaders had become entangled in hair-splitting theological disputes. Those dilemmas created criteria for deciding the quality of a person's religious life and their relationship with God. Puritanism also continued to be strong in the British colonies; however, it lost its original purpose, which was to "purify" the Anglican Church. Instead, it became even more repressive and gave rise to the Salem witch trials in 1692 and 1693. In many ways, it was a recreation of the struggles Anne had gone through with those who didn't permit her to be true to herself. The majority of "witches" were women, and they were labeled as being weak and evil because they didn't conform to the mandates of those who labeled themselves as strong and good—namely, men. Yet, in the world of reality, men and women are not opposites; they are two facets of "human."

Check out another book by Captivating History

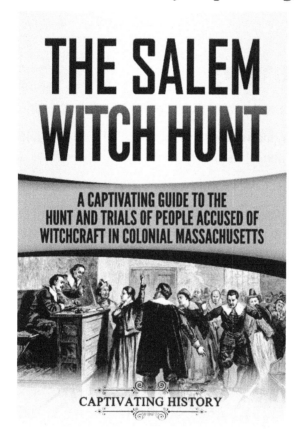

Bibliography

"The Problem with Anne Hutchinson," Retrieved from

https://theimaginativeconservative.org/2019/10/problem-anne-hutchinson-michael-connolly.html

Belknap, M. R. (1994) *American Political Trials* Praeger (2nd edition)

Bradford, W. & Bradford, J. A. *Of Plymouth Plantation, 1620-1647* Retrieved from https://scholarworks.montana.edu/xmlui/bitstream/handle/1/4676/31 762100116936.pdf;sequence=1

Burnham, M. "Anne Hutchinson and the Economics of Antinomian Selfhood in Colonial New England," Retrieved from https://scholarcommons.scu.edu/cgi/viewcontent.cgi?article=1008&context=engl

"Colonial Presbyterianism: Old Faith in a New Land" Retrieved from http://www.centerforcongregationalleadership.com/uploads/6/0/0/9/6 009825/woodward_richard.pdf

Dale, E. (2018) *Debating and Creating – Authority: The Failure of a Constitutional Ideal* Routledge

Hofstadter, R. & Ver Steeg, C.L. (1969) *Great Issues in American History, Vol. 1: From Settlement to Revolution: 1584-1776* Vintage

Glover, J. (2014) *Paper Sovereigns: Anglo-Native Treaties and the Law of Nations, 1604-1664* University of Pennsylvania Press

Jones, M. (2013) *"Antinomianism" Reformed Theology's Unwelcome Guest* R&R Publishing

Kamensky, J. (1999) *Governing the Tongue: The Politics of Speech in Early New England* Oxford University Press

LaPlante, E. (2005) *American Jezebel: The Uncommon Life of Anne Hutchinson, the Woman Who Defied the Puritans* Harper One: Reprint ed.

Leight, J. (2001) "Anne Hutchinson: A Life in Private," The Concord Review, Inc. Winter, 2001

Rowlandson, M. A. (2013 repr.) *True History of the Captivity and Restoration of Mrs. Mary Rowlandson* Alejandro's Libros

Shepard, T. (1853) *The Works of Thomas Shepard: First Pastor of the First Church Cambridge, Mass. With a Memoir of His Life and Character, Vol 1* Doctrinal Tract and Book Society

"Wappinger History," Retrieved from http://www.dickshovel.com/wap.html "Wappinger History"

Winship, M. P. Making Heretics: Militant Protestantism and Free Grace in Massachusetts Retrieved from http://people.ucls.uchicago.edu/~pdoyle/bustlesandbeaux.wordpress.com-Mrs_Hutchinson_by_Nathaniel_Hawthorne1830.pdf

Winship, M. "Times and Trials of Anne Hutchinson," Retrieved from http://historicalsolutions.com/the-times-and-trials-of-anne-hutchinson-by-michael-winship/

Made in the USA
Monee, IL
03 June 2021